YORK NOTES

General Editors: Professor A.N. Jef[...]
of Stirling) & Professor Suheil Bush[...]
University of Beirut)

Plato

THE
REPUBLIC

Notes by Robin Sowerby

MA PH D (CAMBRIDGE)
Lecturer, Department of English Studies,
University of Stirling

LONGMAN
YORK PRESS

YORK PRESS
Immeuble Esseily, Place Riad Solh, Beirut.

LONGMAN GROUP LIMITED
Longman House,
Burnt Mill,
Harlow,
Essex

First published 1985
ISBN 0 582 79225 8
Produced by Longman Group (FE) Ltd
Printed in Hong Kong

Contents

Part 1

Introduction

The life of Plato

Plato was born of aristocratic parents in about 427BC in Athens. He wrote poetry in his youth but abandoned it for philosophy probably when he encountered the philosopher Socrates (469–399BC) who was the major shaping influence upon his life. In the *Republic*, written about 375BC but set in earlier time, the two young men, Glaucon and Adeimantus, with whom Socrates principally conducts his dialogue and whom he enlightens in the course of it are the elder brothers of Plato. Plato himself must have sat at the feet of Socrates and learnt his philosophy in a similar way.

By the time of Plato's birth the great age of Athenian imperialism that began after the Persian wars of the 490s and 480s had reached its zenith under the leadership of Pericles, the most influential statesman in the Athenian democracy from the mid-century till his death in 429BC. Athens went to war with Sparta in 431BC and the war continued in various phases until the defeat of Athens with the consequent loss of her empire in 404BC. The Greek world was divided in support for the leading protagonists, oligarchies and oligarchic parties supporting Sparta, democracies supporting Athens. The successors of Pericles who led the Athenian democracy mismanaged the war, and the Athenian state in its later stages came under the control of an oligarchy in 411, being ruled by the Council of the Four Hundred. This was followed by a further change when for a year the government was in the hands of the Five Thousand, a limited democracy, until full democracy was restored in 410BC with violent measures taken against the oligarchs. After defeat in 404BC there was an oligarchic revolution supported by the Spartans resulting in further tyranny, this time by the oligarchs. Democracy was restored after about a year. For the whole of Plato's youth, therefore, Athens had been at war, and its government in the latter stages of what proved to be a disastrous conflict disastrously managed had been periodically unstable and tyrannous.

After the defeat of Athens came what was undoubtedly a decisive and formative event in Plato's life, the trial and death of Socrates in 399BC. Socrates was accused of introducing strange gods to Athens and demoralising the youth of the city. He was found guilty, condemned to death and drank hemlock in the traditional manner. Thereupon Plato turned aside from the political career he had contemplated, withdrew from Athens to a neighbouring state, Megara, whence he travelled extensively, making contact with the Pythagorean community in southern Italy (see below, p.7) and visiting Syracuse in Sicily. Here he stayed at the court of the tyrant Dionysius I and met the ruler's brother-in-law Dion, with whom he struck up a friendship. In his seventh letter, written to friends of Dion after his death, Plato records that his experience at Athens had convinced him that good government was only possible if philosophers became kings, or if by a miracle kings became philosophers. Dion, as a man who was in a position to have political influence and a friend who was sympathetic to Plato's views, was such a potential philosopher king. After his visit to Syracuse (which he visited three times) Plato returned to Athens and began teaching in a school situated in the grove of a hero named Academus, whence the school was called the Academy. It seems he hoped that the Academy could be a nursery for philosopher kings, and the school attracted sons of the powerful and wealthy from all over the Greek world. When Dionysius I died in 367BC, Dion invited Plato back to Syracuse to train the new young ruler Dionysius II. But he was not a responsive pupil. Plato's most famous pupil was not a politician but the philosopher Aristotle (384–322BC) who was associated with Plato at the Academy for twenty years until Plato's death in 347BC.

Greek thinkers before Plato

The very word philosophy, meaning in Greek literally the love of wisdom, suggests what the world owes to the early thinkers of Greece. When they wrote the history of their own philosophical development the Greeks normally started with the philosophers of Ionia of the seventh and sixth centuries who were the first Greeks consciously to reject the account of the world handed down in traditional myths and stories in favour of a new kind of speculative enquiry into the nature of the physical universe. Perhaps the movement from myth to philosophy was made easier by the nature of the Greek myths themselves. In the oldest surviving text of Greek culture, the *Iliad* attributed to the epic poet Homer and probably composed more than a century before the earliest of the Ionian philosophers, the king of the gods, Zeus, while being the most powerful of the gods, is not omnipotent or omniscient; nor did he create the world. He shares his power with other gods and himself took power from his father. He is subject to laws beyond his own will. As much as he wishes to save his mortal son from the hands of the enemy he is unable to do so, recognising that he too must submit to fate (*Iliad*, XVI, 433–61). Gods and men alike are subject to a binding necessity. Greek myth as we have it in Homer reflects rather than explains the perplexing nature of things.

The early history of Greek thought is not easy to chart with any certainty because our knowledge of it comes largely from much later accounts which sometimes contradict one another, and from fragments attributed to the philosophers themselves that are sometimes so fragmentary that they are difficult to piece together and make little sense out of their original context, now forever lost. Furthermore, where there are schools of thought that take their origin from a founding father (like the Pythagoreans) and have a continued existence over a long period, it is not always easy to distinguish the original thought from subsequent development of it by succeeding generations. What follows here is designed simply to indicate stages in early Greek thought that have a particular bearing upon Plato.

By common consent the earliest Ionian thinker was Thales of Miletus who was born in the latter half of the seventh century. He believed that the primary substance from which everything came into being and of which all is ultimately made is water. Other Ionian philosophers asking the same questions came to different conclusions about the primordial substance. But their common enquiry was into the nature of the physical universe on the assumption that it is both one and intelligible.

The philosopher Pythagoras in the second half of the sixth century marks a reaction against the materialism of the early Ionians. He migrated from Samos in Ionia to southern Italy where he founded a community for initiates on religious lines. Plato refers to their way of life in the *Republic* (600b). Associated with Pythagoras is the doctrine of the soul's immortality and its reincarnation in a cycle of lives in the animal and human spheres (metempsychosis). Accordingly his followers abstained from the eating of flesh. The body is regarded as the prison or tomb of the soul which may be purified in an ascetic life of study. Like the Ionians he sought a single primordial principle by which to explain the universe, but in Pythagoras's thought this was non-material. He explained the universe not in physical but in metaphysical terms tracing the origin of all things to number. He is accredited with developments in the study of mathematics and music. The intervals between the heavenly bodies were supposed to be determined by the laws of musical harmony. Hence arose the doctrine of the harmony of the spheres which in their motion were supposed to make a heavenly music (*Republic*, 617c). With Pythagoras the word *kosmos* which means good order or decency in early Greek is first used to describe the perfect order and arrangement of the universe. At the end of the *Republic* Plato uses Pythagorean imagery in the myth of Er (614– 21), and the second stage of his educational programme based on the study of arithmetic, geometry, harmonics, and astronomy is of Pythagorean inspiration (524d–531c).

Another early thinker who influenced the development of the whole course of subsequent Greek philosophy is Heraclitus of Ephesus who lived in the late sixth and early fifth centuries and was nicknamed 'the obscure' because of the difficulty of his prose, fragments of which survive in quotations in other authors. In his work *On Nature* he expressed the belief that fire is the primordial substance. The world is an everlasting fire which is partly flaring up and partly dying down in equal measure so that a continuous balance is maintained. Essential to this balance are tension and strife in which all subsists. Unlike other Ionian materialists he associated this primordial element with the *Logos* (in Greek this means word or reason) which governed the existence of the everlasting fire. The *Logos* is to be identified with what is eternal and constant, the One, while the phenomenal world is constantly changing and in a state of flux. It is not possible to step into the same river twice and there is a new sun every day (*Republic*, 498). This universal reason, the principle by which there is unity in diversity and diversity in unity, is divine and all-wise. Man can understand the *Logos* by virtue of a spark of the *Logos* within, that is, human reason. The business of life is to harmonise the *Logos* within man with the universal *Logos*. Man must therefore seek to understand and accept his place in the order of the world which is governed by the necessity of universal law. Here is the beginning of the philosophical conception of the life according to reason and nature.

A third major development in early Greek philosophy emanated from the Eleatic school (Elea was a Greek colony in southern Italy) and is associated with the fifth-century philosopher Parmenides. He expressed his philosophical convictions in a didactic poem *On Nature*. He believed that Being, the One, is real while Becoming, change, is illusion. He argued that if anything comes into existence, it must come out of being or out of not being. If it comes from being, then it already is; if it comes from nothing then it is itself nothing since nothing can come to be out of nothing. Becoming, change, and plurality are therefore illusory. He distinguished two ways of apprehending the world. There is the way of truth, in which there is knowledge of being, and the way of opinion (the common condition of ordinary men and women) that takes the world of becoming as real. The mutable world of appearances that we apprehend through the senses is unreal; being is the only true object of knowledge and is known through reason and thought. This distinction is basic to Plato's philosophy, though there is a crucial difference between Plato and Parmenides. Parmenides seems to have believed that being is material while for Plato being is non-material, that is ideal.

Socrates

With Socrates the course of Greek philosophy takes a new turn. The Ionians had been largely concerned with rational enquiry into the physical nature of the universe. Socrates may have begun by thinking about physics, but he soon turned directly to ethics, to thought about human conduct and moral behaviour. This definite new direction is marked by the name given to all thinkers before Socrates who are known collectively as the pre-Socratics. The Roman writer Cicero (106–43 BC) made the famous remark that Socrates first brought philosophy down from the skies to the common problems of mankind (*Tusculan Disputations*, V, 4, 10).

Socrates himself did not write anything so that our knowledge of him comes principally from two sources, from Plato himself, who featured Socrates in his dialogues, and from the historian Xenophon (*c*.428/7– *c*.354 BC), who wrote recollections of Socrates in his *Memorabilia*. What is clear from their evidence is summed up succinctly by Aristotle, who records that Socrates taught inductive reasoning and was concerned with universal definitions (*Metaphysics*, 1078b).

What Aristotle's cold summary means in practice can be demonstrated from the manner in which Plato makes Socrates conduct his argument in the opening stage of the *Republic*. One of the participants in the dialogue, Polemarchus, puts forward the conventional proposition that justice or right conduct consists in giving every man what is due to him. Socrates makes Polemarchus explain what he means and at each stage of his explanation brings forward particular instances which show that the formulations of Polemarchus are inadequate. Eventually Socrates forces Polemarchus to admit that he does not know what he really means at all (344b). In this way the inductive reasoning (that is, the use of particular instances to lead to general conclusion) is used to destroy what is considered to be an inadequate definition of justice or at least an inadequate defence of it by Polemarchus. Polemarchus is forced onto the defensive and made to think about the words he uses and about what it is that he really means. Later in the *Republic* Socrates concerns himself positively with the construction of an argument that leads to a universal definition of justice, so that the Socrates of the *Republic* is what we should expect him to be in the light of Aristotle's summary.

This way of proceeding was for Socrates a divine mission. In his *Apology*, an early dialogue, Plato has Socrates tell how his friend Chaerophon had consulted the oracle at Delphi to ask whether there was anyone wiser than Socrates. The oracle replied 'No'. Dumbfounded at this, Socrates set out to refute the oracle by seeking out those with reputations for wisdom, philosophers, poets and skilled craftsmen, only to find that they knew nothing at all but unlike Socrates did not recognise their own ignorance. Thereafter he considered that it was his duty to disabuse all sorts and conditions of men of their own self-ignorance and so put them on the road to truth. His favourite method involved cross-questioning; for this he pretended to be ignorant in order to draw out and then refute an opponent. The Greek word for this kind of pretence is *eironeia*, and this questioning method is called Socratic irony (*Republic*, 337a). The refutation is generally called the *elenchus* which is the word for refutation in Greek. The *elenchus*, by destroying the conceit that we already know, arouses the desire to know, supplying the motive lacking before. The *elenchus* is therefore personal in character. The answerer must believe in his own primary statement and must be convinced of the logical validity of the argument whose premises he must genuinely accept. Hence the argument must proceed by agreement. The essence of the *elenchus* lies in making visible to the answerer the contradiction between certain of his actual beliefs and the nature of his present thesis. The *elenchus* is negative in effect, destructive of self-ignorance, conventional beliefs and received opinions; the first effect of it is perplexity or impasse, *aporia* in Greek. But as an instrument of the probing intelligence of Socrates it served a positive moral function in clearing the way for positive definitions and clarity of thought about moral issues, about the value and end of human conduct.

How far the historical Socrates is to be identified with the constructive thought of Plato has long been a matter for debate. There is no reason to believe that Plato felt constrained by the need to preserve literal historical accuracy in his portrayal of Socrates in his dialogues, which were all written sometime after Socrates's death. The historian Thucydides (*c.*460–*c.*400BC), for example, invents speeches for leading figures like Pericles in his history of *The Peloponnesian War* according to his general notion of what it was likely they might have said, given the needs of the occasion (I, 22). The commonest belief among scholars is that Socrates did not develop any system of belief and that the theory of forms, for example, was Plato's development of tendencies in Socrates's thinking. It is generally agreed that Socrates concerned himself first and foremost with the method by which truth is to be sought. Put simply, he wished to train people to think.

In a famous analogy Plato makes Socrates compare his mission in life to that of his mother who was a midwife. He can deliver truth to those who come to him, but the labour and the pains are theirs; the truth is to be born through them:

> I am so far like the midwife that I cannot myself give birth to wisdom, and the common reproach is true, that, though I question others, I can myself bring nothing to light because there is no wisdom in me. The reason is this. Heaven constrains me to serve as a midwife, but has debarred me from giving birth. So of myself I have no sort of wisdom, nor has any discovery ever been born to me as the child of my soul. Those who frequent my company at first appear,

some of them, quite unintelligent, but as we go further with our discussions, all who are favoured by heaven make progress at a rate that seems surprising to others as well as to themselves, although it is clear that they have never learned anything from me. The many admirable truths they bring to birth have been discovered by themselves from within. But the delivery is heaven's work and mine.... Accept, then, the ministration of a midwife's son who himself practises his mother's art, and do the best you can to answer the questions I ask. Perhaps when I examine your statements I may judge one or another of them to be an unreal phantom. If I then take the abortion from you and cast it away, do not be savage with me like a woman robbed of her first child. People have often felt like that toward me and been positively ready to bite me for taking away some foolish notion they have conceived. They do not see that I am doing them a kindness. They have not learned that no divinity is ever ill-disposed towards man, nor is such action on my part due to unkindness; it is only that I am not permitted to acquiesce in falsehood and suppress the truth.*

(*Theaetetus*, 150c, 151b)

This is not the method of one who, like earlier philosophers, seeks to impart truth from without; he works to make each individual mind seek the ground of its own conviction.

The doctrine which seems to have been the ground of Socrates's ethical beliefs is expressed in the proposition that virtue is knowledge. The wise man who knows what is good and what conduces to human happiness will do what is good and conduces to human happiness. Wrong actions are a result of a faulty perception of what conduces to true human good. It is possible to learn (and therefore to teach) what conduces to true human good and happiness, and once learnt the knowledge will be irresistible. Hence it is possible to say that no one willingly does wrong.

The doctrine that virtue is knowledge acquired a particular authority from the character of Socrates himself who seemed to his contemporaries its very embodiment. We probably have a fuller characterisation of Socrates than of any other ancient Greek. He has always been looked upon as the supreme exemplar of pagan virtue. Not that his goodness makes him a saintly figure in quite the usual sense of the word. Nor is his virtue expressed in an entirely typical Greek form. Greek excellence was ideally a blend of physical and intellectual qualities. The poise and balance of the Greek ideal is represented in the sculpture of the classical

---

* In the translation by F.M. Cornford in *The Collected Dialogues of Plato*, edited by Edith Hamilton and Huntingdon Cairns, Princeton University Press, Princeton, N.J., 1961, pp.855–6.

period and in the idealised portraits in stone that survive of the great philosophers and men of letters such as Aristotle of Thucydides. In flesh and blood Socrates was fat, ungainly, snub-nosed and ugly. He was a jolly figure who amused his companions, who likened him in jest to the mythical figure of Silenus, a pot-bellied, sleep-prone drunkard who in sober waking moments dispensed wisdom to those who could pin him down and constrain him to do so. Into this comic portrait fits the figure of his wife Xanthippe, an archetypal shrew who gave her husband a bad time. Through Plato's dialogues Socrates is associated with drinking parties where it is said he could outdrink the best. He is the ideal boon companion. The drinking party or *Symposium* is the setting and title for what is after the *Republic* Plato's most famous dialogue, on the nature of love. In this setting is an extended eulogy of Socrates (*Symposium*, 215–20). Socrates is therefore no ascetic. He enjoyed the things of the world, chief amongst which was good conversation in congenial company, 'the feast of reason and the flow of soul', where wine and friendship flowed in equal measure. This fully human setting is what has given the Socratic method its irresistible appeal. Socrates's love of knowledge and his desire to lead others to knowledge is inseparably bound up with his love of his fellow men and his practical human concern.

Nevertheless the dialogue which shows Socrates in his most famous setting also records the abstract reverie into which Socrates fell when making his way to the drinking party (*Symposium*, 175). Socrates was renowned for his moments of withdrawal from the world and for the depth of his inward concentration. Although he greatly enjoyed life, he is lauded for his great self-control and for his essential indifference to the needs of the senses. In the *Symposium* it is said that whatever his capacity for wine Socrates had never been drunk (220). He lived simply, and his defenders emphasise his obedience to the laws of his country which he served with courage and distinction in war. Despite the charges brought against him, he had respect for the state religion and was a god-fearing man with a more developed theological sense than his contemporaries. He interpreted the inner voice which gave him a warning sign (*Republic*, 496c) as being of divine origin, and his mission of self-examination and the cross-examination of others he also regarded as being laid upon him by divine command:

> Perhaps someone may say, but surely, Socrates, after you have left us you can spend the rest of your life in quietly minding your own business. This is the hardest thing of all to make some of you understand. If I say that this would be disobedience to god, and that is why I cannot 'mind my own business' you will not believe that I am serious. If on the other hand I tell you that to let no day pass without

discussing goodness and all the other subjects about which you hear me talking and examining both myself and others is really the very best thing that a man can do, and that life without this sort of examination is not worth living, you will be even less inclined to believe me*
(*Apology*, 37e)

At his trial he refused to employ a proper defence (see the oblique reference to this at *Republic*, 517d), simply making an honest avowal of his life's aims and endeavours. When convicted he refused to escape from prison, and showed true courage and true philosophic calm when facing death. For Xenophon he was the best and happiest of men; pious, just, self-controlled, sensible (*Memorabilia*, 1, 11). After recounting his death in his dialogue, the *Phaedo*, Plato pronounces him to have been of all whom they knew in their time, the best, the wisest and the most upright man (*Phaedo*, 118). Plato's tribute culminates in the superlative form of the adjective *dikaios*, (here rendered as upright) which is related to the noun *dikaiosyne*, 'justice' or 'righteousness', the sum of the four cardinal virtues of the ancient world and the subject of the *Republic*. In his life and in the manner of his dying Socrates embodied for his age the perfection of the philosophic spirit.

The sophists

The philosophical method of Socrates is one of the fruits of the great intellectual change that manifested itself throughout the Greek-speaking world in the second half of the fifth century, sometimes known as the Greek enlightenment. The same period saw the growth of a new kind of professional teacher throughout Greece. These men were called sophists, a name derived from the Greek word for wisdom or skill, *sophia*. They moved from city to city and gave lessons for money in such matters as mathematics, politics and the art of public speaking. They aimed to give a practical education whereby the rising middle classes might be successful in public life.

The Athenian comedian Aristophanes (*c*. 450–*c*.385 BC) satirises the sophists in his play the *Clouds*, produced in 423 BC, and chooses Socrates as the representative of the new learning. An elderly farmer called Strepsiades has heard of Socrates, a man who can make the worse cause appear the better one, and hopes to profit by his teaching to cheat those to whom he is in debt. He goes to the 'thinking school' of Socrates where he is introduced to the clouds whom Socrates alleges to be responsible for producing the rain rather than Zeus. But Strepsiades is too stupid to learn anything so he sends his son Pheidippides instead.

* Translated by Hugh Tredennick in *The Collected Dialogues of Plato*, pp.22–3.

Pheidippides hears the unjust argument defeat the just argument, and as a result of his new learning he is able to teach his father to cheat his creditors. But he then beats his father, proving in argument that he is justified in doing so and disowns the authority of the gods. Strepsiades sets fire to Socrates's school in disgust.

Socrates is here ridiculed for what he was charged with in court, and for what he was condemned to death in 399BC, namely introducing strange gods into Athens and corrupting the morals of the young. Doubtless Aristophanes was exploiting a confusion that existed in the public mind between Socrates and those who were thought to have undermined traditional morality, as a result of which it could be argued Athens had been defeated in the Peloponnesian War. In fact Socrates never set up a school, nor did he take fees for instruction. Conversely there is no evidence that the sophists shared Socrates's methods. Plato draws a sharp distinction between Socrates and the sophists whom he generally represents as men who taught skills without any genuine interest in moral truth or in the ends which knowledge should be made to serve. Plato's hostility is apparent in his portrayal of Thrasymachus in the opening stages of the *Republic* (see also his direct comment at 492).

A note on the text

There have been countless editions of Plato since the first edition printed in 1513. A notable edition is that of Stephanus (1578) whose page numbers (subdivided from a to e) are conventionally used in subsequent editions and translations to divide the text for common reference. A standard modern edition of the Greek text of the *Republic* can be found in *Plato*, Vol. IV, edited by J. Burnet, Oxford Classical Texts, Clarendon Press, Oxford, 1962.

Part 2

Summaries
of THE REPUBLIC

A general summary

The dialogue begins with an enquiry into the nature of justice (right conduct, morality, 'righteousness') in which Socrates refutes conventional views of justice, in particular that put forward by Polemarchus, who says that justice is a matter of giving every man his due. The sophist Thrasymachus then asserts that justice is the interest of the stronger, that successful self-aggrandisement is the true principle of life and that injustice and freedom from restraint and law lead to greater happiness than justice. Socrates is able to silence Thrasymachus by abstract arguments but admits that he is not satisfied because he has not given a positive definition of true justice (Book One ends here). Glaucon and Adeimantus restate the view of Thrasymachus and challenge Socrates to prove that justice pays better than injustice and is intrinsically desirable. Socrates begins his answer by proposing that they examine justice and injustice in the community where they are easier to see on a large scale before moving to the individual. He proposes to examine society in its most elementary form to find the origin of justice. Society develops because the individual is not self-sufficient. Through the principle of the division of labour mutual need is satisfied. When the simplest social unit becomes more sophisticated with a desire for the amenities of civilised life, more territory is needed, and this results in war, for which a defence force of guardian soldiers will be necessary. If these guardians are not to be aggressive in their behaviour to each other and to the rest of the community they must have a philosophic disposition to temper their spirit and physical strength. This leads on to a discussion of the kind of education by which this is to be achieved so that here begin the prescriptions for the ideal state.

The early education of the guardians will be divided into two parts, one embracing the artistic and literary and the other embracing the physical. Only poetry that is morally and theologically sound will be read, and only simple and noble musical styles and instruments will be allowed to ensure that aesthetic development and a strong moral sense run parallel. Physical education is not an end in itself but is to strengthen character, providing the necessary balance so that the guardians will be both philosophic and spirited. The best of them will rule the state. The rest will be auxiliaries and have executive power carrying out the orders of the guardians and directing the third class of artisans and craftsmen. The citizens must be persuaded of the truth of a foundation myth for the sake of social identity and unity. The guardians and auxiliaries will have no private property and will hold all things in common with their material needs provided for by the rest of the citizens. Further duties are laid down for the guardians.

The ideal state will embody the four cardinal virtues of wisdom, courage, temperance and justice. Its wisdom will reside in the guardians, its courage in the auxiliaries and its temperance in the harmonious acceptance of the order of the state by all three classes. Justice is the principle that makes this temperance possible; it is an extension of the principle of the division of labour upon which society is based in the first place, the principle whereby each class fulfils its own function without trespassing upon the functions of the other two. The argument moves from the state to the individual. The individual soul is made up of three parts corresponding to the three classes in the state; the rational part, the spirited part and the appetitive part. The wisdom of the individual resides in the rational part, courage in the spirited part and temperance in the harmonious relation between the three parts, specifically in the way in which the lower parts consent to the rule of reason. Justice in the individual as in the state is the principle whereby this temperance is possible, the principle whereby each part of the soul fulfils its own function without interfering with the operation of the other two. Justice is therefore the harmony and health of the soul.

Socrates has now offered a positive definition of justice and proposes to demonstrate that justice is intrinsically better than injustice by comparing the ideal state with various forms of the unjust state. Here Adeimantus interrupts, wishing to know more about the community of women and children briefly referred to earlier. After a declaration about the equality of women Socrates lays down provisions for relations between the sexes and the begetting of children, and then for the conduct of war and military training, when he is interrupted by Glaucon who asks whether all these provisions are practicable. Socrates argues that this is a secondary consideration which does not affect the soundness of the enquiry into the nature of true justice, but declares that the least change necessary to bring about the ideal state is for rulers to become philosophers. He then defines what he means by a philosopher and discusses the charge that philosophers are useless and often dangerous. The true philosopher looks beyond the particularities of the phenomenal world that is perceived by the senses, to a higher order of reality.

On the basis that the guardians must be philosophers Socrates begins to consider further educational provision for their intellectual development. The ultimate end of this education is knowledge of the good.

When pressed to define this, Socrates confesses that he is unable to do so, proceeding instead by analogy, using the simile of the sun, the figure of the divided line and the allegory of the cave. The guardians must have further education beyond that described earlier which had been designed to promote harmonious development of character rather than to reach true knowledge. They will be exercised in various branches of mathematics, astronomy, and harmonics not for any practical value but purely for the training of the mind. Those who are successful in this will study dialectic through which they may arrive at knowledge of the good. They will then be true philosophers ready to rule the state.

Having completed his account of the ideal state, Socrates takes up the argument where he had left it at the end of Book Four, and proceeds to describe various forms of injustice in the state and in the individual. Four main types of unjust state are analysed; timocracy, oligarchy, democracy and tyranny. Following the description of each state is an account of the timocratic individual, the oligarch, the democrat and the tyrant. Socrates then ranks these states and individuals in order of happiness, finding the tyrant the least happy of all and juxtaposing him with the philosopher ruler in order to refute the claims of Thrasymachus which initiated the enquiry into justice in the first place. Even if the ideal state cannot be realised on earth, the philosopher can so order his life that he finds the pattern of it in himself.

Finally Socrates returns to the subject of poetry and gives reasons for excluding all but hymns to the gods and eulogies of good men from the ideal state. He goes on to describe the rewards that goodness can win which leads him to argue for the immortality of the soul. The dialogue ends with the myth of Er.

Detailed summaries

Book One

Socrates and Glaucon go down to the Piraeus to see a festival in honour of the goddess Bendis when they meet Polemarchus, Adeimantus, Niceratus and others who take them to the house of Cephalus, the father of Polemarchus. Cephalus, an old man who has led a good and successful life, has a conversation with Socrates on the subject of old age in the course of which Socrates asks him what he thinks justice is (right conduct) and then questions whether his comments on the subject can be an adequate answer. Cephalus excuses himself from the conversation to go and make sacrifice and Polemarchus continues on his behalf. He quotes a definition of right conduct given by the poet Simonides: that it is a matter of giving every man his due. Socrates shows the inadequacy of this formulation, which is then further defined to the effect that right conduct means doing good to our friends, those whom we regard as men of integrity, and harm to our enemies. Socrates undermines this definition with the assertion that we are often deceived in our judgment of people. Polemarchus restates the proposition of Simonides to the effect that it is right to help our friends if they are good men and to injure our enemies if they are bad. Socrates argues that harming men makes them less good, and asks how this can itself be right. Here the sophist Thrasymachus takes up the argument, dismissing conventional views of justice and morality and arguing that right is the interest of the stronger. In all states it is considered wrong to break the law; the law is enacted by those who rule and the government is stronger than its subjects, so that moral behaviour is what is exacted from the weaker by the stronger. Socrates objects that rulers often make mistakes about their own interests so that the subject who must rightly obey the law often acts against the true interests of the stronger. Thrasymachus replies that rulers as rulers never make mistakes. If they do, they cannot properly be called rulers. Socrates shows that every art, including the art of government, looks to the interests not of the practitioners like the doctor but to those for whom it is practised, the patients. Against this abstract argument, Thrasymachus, appealing to experience, argues that a ruler treats his subjects like a shepherd who fattens his flock for his own private interest. Socrates refutes this saying that the shepherd, as shepherd, looks to the good of his sheep. Socrates then turns to a central question raised by the arguments of Thrasymachus. Is successful self-aggrandisement the true principle of life? Does injustice pay better than justice or right conduct? Socrates again uses the analogy of the skilled practitioner. If a doctor has treated a patient correctly, another doctor will not seek to outdo him in his treatment. Similarly, the good man excels the immoral man but is not in competition with other good men. If each individual strives to outdo everyone else, there will be strife, dissension, and incapacity for joint action. Finally on the basis that the virtue of the soul is justice, Socrates argues that only right conduct can lead to true happiness. Nevertheless Socrates is dissatisfied because he has not found a positive definition of the real nature of justice.

NOTES AND GLOSSARY:

Piraeus: (327. For an explanation of the bracketed references see 'A note on the text' p.14.) the harbour of Athens, five miles from the city

Glaucon and Adeimantus: elder brothers of Plato

the festival: in honour of Bendis, a Thracian goddess (Thrace is in northern Greece) identified with Artemis, the moon goddess, and goddess of chastity and hunting

Lysias: (328b) (459–380BC) a famous orator

Chalcedon: (328b) on the Bosphorus. Thrasymachus is therefore a distinguished foreigner, as is Charmantides from Paeania in northern Greece. All the characters of Plato's dialogues are historical persons and include some of the most notable thinkers in the Greek world

Sophocles: (329c) lived to a great age (496–406BC). His most famous play is *King Oedipus*. Though written about 375BC the *Republic* is thought to have been set at the earlier time of about 420BC

Themistocles: (329e) (528–462BC) a prominent Athenian leader in the wars against Persia in the 480s. Seriphus is a small island in the Aegean Sea

Pindar: (331) (518–438BC) a lyric poet who wrote odes in celebration of victors at the Greek games. It is characteristic of the older generation to appeal to the authority of the old poets

right conduct: (331c) Plato's word *dikaiosyne*, often translated as justice, has a wider meaning embracing right conduct and what is morally good. The alternative title given to the *Republic* in antiquity is 'About *dikaiosyne*'

Polemarchus: (331d) son of Cephalus. His idea of justice is not like that of his father, based upon experience, but is a conventional notion accepted from tradition that he does not wholly understand, and that proves to be an inadequate definition

Simonides: (331d) (556–468BC) a lyric and elegiac poet. In pre-philosophic Greece poets were regarded as authorities on matters of conduct and morals

justice and human excellence: (335c) the Greek word *arete* is sometimes translated goodness or virtue. It has the meaning of excellence in whatever context it is found; it is the *arete* of a knife to cut well

Bias or Pittacus: (335e) poets who lived a hundred years before Plato and were among the seven sages of Greece. Among the others were Thales the Milesian philosopher and Solon the Athenian lawgiver. Traditional 'wisdom' is again shown to be inadequate

Periander, Xerxes: (336) proverbial tyrants. A Socratic joke

Thrasymachus: (336b) a sophist, that is, a professional teacher (who took fees), offering a practical education, the corner stone of which was usually the art of rhetoric and public speaking. He is a caricature of the 'worldly wise'

Thrasymachus rebukes Socrates: (336c) this method of asking questions from a position of feigned ignorance was a favourite technique of Socrates in argument with the sophists. Later, at 337c, Thrasymachus again accuses Socrates of using his customary *eironeia*, dissimulation. The sophist is pompous and vain. His irascibility and his inability to cope with Socrates in argument make him to some extent a comic figure

Book Two

Glaucon and Adeimantus express dissatisfaction with the way in which Socrates has dealt with the argument of Thrasymachus, which they restate in a new form. Glaucon argues that justice or morality is a compact of convenience. All men will naturally like to pursue their own interests and commit acts of injustice if they can be sure of getting away with them, and of not suffering injustice from other men in return. But few are strong enough to do this, so that laws are made in the interests of the majority to protect them from injustice. Morality is a consequence, therefore, of our fear of injustice. Furthermore, justice is not intrinsically valuable because one who merely appears to be upright but is in fact the very opposite may have or acquire all the good things in life while the truly just man may suffer abominably. Adeimantus argues that men only value justice for the reward it brings in terms of good reputation in society, and in the world beyond for the gods reward the just. On the other hand people believe that right conduct is difficult and that wrong-doing pays better. In this they are encouraged by contemporary prophets who offer them means of avoiding punishment in this world by making sacrifices and in the next through the appropriate initiation ceremonies. Socrates is then asked to show how justice or right conduct is desirable for the individual not for the rewards it brings with it, but intrinsically for its own sake.

Socrates begins by proposing that they consider justice in the community on the assumption that the life of the state is the life of the men composing it on a larger scale, which is therefore easier to observe and describe. Socrates will then proceed from the state to the individual. He proposes to examine the origin of justice and injustice in the most elementary society (giving not an actual history but a logical account). Society comes to be because no man is self-sufficient. Men have different talents and capacities which result in the division of labour. Accordingly society is a natural development to the advantage of all its individual members. Socrates then sketches the growth of a rudimentary social organisation. First there will be farmers, builders, weavers, and shoe-makers, then carpenters, smiths, shepherds, cowmen, and stockmen. Then with foreign trade will come merchants and sailors. There will be retailers, a currency, shops and hired labourers. Glaucon protests that such a society is uncivilised. To the necessities of existence are now added the luxuries of civilised life. There will be a desire for confection-ery, furniture, call girls, actors, poets, cosmetics, painting, embroidery, and so on. The desire for luxury and an increase in population will lead to the need for more territory and consequently to war. Soldiers and guardians will be necessary to fight for and protect the state. How are these guardians to be selected and what qualities must they have? They must be strong, courageous, high-spirited, yet gentle and of a philoso-phic disposition. How are they to be educated? In childhood great care must be taken over the content of the stories they are told. Most exist-ing poetry is to be avoided because it gives a false idea of the gods who are perfectly good and therefore do not change form or mislead us by deceit as they are represented as doing by the poets.

NOTES AND GLOSSARY:

Glaucon on justice: the first philosophical statement of the theory of the social contract

Gyges the Lydian: (359c) the kingdom of Lydia was in Asia Minor, far south of Troy. The historian Heredotus (*c*.495 – *c*.425BC) also tells his story in his *Histories*, 1, 8 – 12

Aeschylus: (361b) the famous tragic writer (525 – 456BC), much venerated in Plato's day as a classic play-wright of the Athenian heroic age. The quotation is from his *Seven against Thebes*, lines 593 – 4

Adeimantus on justice: (362d) argues that justice is recommended for the reputation it brings by all parents, teachers, and educators who cite the authority of the poets. Socrates will attack the poets for being inadequate moral guides at the end of the book

Hesiod: (363) (*c*.700BC) author of a didactic poem on the origin and nature of the gods, the *Theogony*, and of a didactic poem on life and work called the *Works and Days*. He was another venerated ancient authority. The quotation here is from *Works and Days*, 232 and 287

Homer: (363) (*c*.9th – 8th century BC); every Greek school-boy read Homer and learned passages by heart. He is the author of the epic poems, the *Iliad* and the

Odyssey, from which Plato cites a number of passages, particularly in the discussion of poetry in Books Two, Three and Ten. The most venerated poet, 'the educator of Greece': see 606c. His gods are notoriously immoral and often comic; his heroes are passionate and from Plato's viewpoint uncontrolled and 'unphilosophic'. The quotations here are from *Odyssey*, XIX, 109 and *Iliad*, IX, 497

Musaeus: (363c) a mythical singer; oracles and poems on the Orphic mysteries were attributed to him

Orpheus: (364e) another mythical poet, supposedly the founder of Orphism, an archaic religious movement

the Muses: (364e) nine in number, the daughters of Zeus, king of the gods, and Memory. They presided over the various arts

Pindar: (365b) see the notes to the previous book. Like the other poets cited here, a poet of the heroic past

Archilochus: (365c) a lyric poet of the seventh century. He is the author of a famous saying 'The fox knows many things; the hedgehog one great thing' (compare 423d)

justice in the community: (368c) Plato's word is *polis* (whence politics), the Greek city state. Justice is to be found on a larger scale here. This is a crucial point in the argument

the primitive society: (369) there may be irony in Socrates's description of it as a happy state; it is the lowest order of the civilised state. Slavery is taken for granted. Note that Plato considers society entirely natural and necessary

developed society: (372d) in this there is satire directed against the luxurious society of contemporary Athens. Compare 399 where Socrates speaks of purging society of its luxurious excess. In the developed society unnecessary occupations proliferate

war: (373e) that the ideal state should come into existence as a result of the need to make provision for war has occasioned much comment

watchdogs: (375) the guardians, as their name implies, are to defend the state. Thereafter they are to be the major focus of Plato's attention. Little mention is made subsequently of the lower orders of society

the guardians must be philosophical: (375e) a crucial point in the development of the argument

the education of the guardians: (376e) the first stage. Further education will be described in Book Seven, 521c–541c. The first part of Plato's prescriptions relates to education in all the arts that come under the diréction of the Muses, that is principally to literature and music. The Greek word to express all this is *mousike* which has no direct equivalent in English

Ouranos: (377e) the sky god, the first ruler of the gods who was castrated by his son Cronos who in turn was deposed by Zeus with the help of the Titans, divine giants

the battle of the Giants: (378c) they fought with Zeus and the Olympian gods and were defeated by them

Hera and Hephaestus: (378d) Hera is the wife of Zeus and mother of Hephaestus: see *Iliad*, I, 586–94

Homer's battles of the gods: (378d) they fight each other in *Iliad*, XX and XXI. Allegorical interpretation of the mythological tradition was well established by the time of Plato

Zeus and the fates: (379d) from the great speech of Achilles, hero of the *Iliad*, at XXIV, 527. For Plato god (or the gods) is good and cannot dispense good and evil randomly as suggested in Homer's image

Athene, Zeus and Pandarus: (379e) this occurs in *Iliad*, IV, 69

Themis and Zeus: (379e) *Iliad*, XX, 1–74

Niobe: (380) she had six sons and six daughters. She boasted that she was superior to Leto who had only two children, Apollo and Artemis. They killed all her children for her presumption

the house of Pelops: (380) was afflicted by a succession of crimes and calamities. Atreus, son of Pelops, killed the sons of his brother Thyestes and served them up to him for dinner. Atreus's son Agamemnon sacrificed his daughter Iphigeneia to Artemis, and was himself murdered by his wife Clytemnestra. She in turn was murdered by her son Orestes. This is the subject of the trilogy of Aeschylus called the *Oresteia*

the Trojan war: (380) the subject of Homer's *Iliad*

Proteus: (381d) a sea god who could change himself into many shapes: hence the adjective Protean

Thetis: (381d) mother of Achilles; a sea goddess, she took many shapes to avoid being given in marriage to the mortal Peleus

Zeus sends Agamemnon a false dream: (383) in *Iliad*, II, 1–34. Agamemnon was leader of the Greeks at Troy

Book Three

Most poetry must be avoided because it may encourage moral weakness such as the fear of death, lack of self-control or undue emotional display. Gods and heroes must not be shown in a bad light. In addition to content care must be taken over the form which poetry takes. Fiction may take three forms, that which is purely imitative such as the drama, that in which the poet speaks in his own person such as the lyric, and that which uses both methods such as the epic. As individuals cannot do or imitate many things successfully they must not be allowed to imitate in their recitations the characters of women, slaves, cowards or unworthy characters using abusive language. Only those works in which the representational element is minimal will be allowed. Poets will be employed to represent the good man in a simple and severe style for imitation by our ruling class. Similarly in music only those styles and instruments which are of a simple and noble character are to be permitted. The soft and relaxing strains of drinking songs, for example, are to be excluded. This stage of education is to develop character alongside an appreciation of beauty, harmony and proportion. Physical education is a vital part of training. A simple and moderate diet will keep the guardians healthy. The educated man ought to have control of his own life, both physically and morally, and should not ordinarily need to consult doctors any more than he should have to go to a court of law. The object of physical education is to develop the energy and the spirit of the individual, and this must be tempered by literary and musical training which is to develop the philosophic side of man. Too much emphasis on the physical produces hardness and brutality; too much emphasis on literature and music produces softness and effeminacy. The ideal is a harmonious blend of both physical and cultural education.

The best of the guardians will be the sovereign rulers in the state; they will be selected by rigorous tests. They will be the oldest, the wisest, the most principled and have the good of the community at heart in all things. The rest will be their auxiliaries who will have executive power in the state. To encourage social cohesion, the people and the guardians themselves must be persuaded of the truth of a splendid myth to the effect that they were all fashioned and reared in the depths of the earth, their common mother, so that they are all brothers of the same parent whom they are bound to protect. The god who made them mixed gold in the composition of the rulers, silver in the auxiliaries, and iron and bronze in the other workers. The first commandment of the gods to the rulers is to preserve the separation of metals in the various classes. Any child of a ruler with a taint of iron or bronze must be degraded to the rank of craftsman. The state will be ruined when it has rulers of silver or bronze. The rulers and auxiliaries must live in a special camp, in a location suitable for the defence of the city, quartered in tents, not houses, without private property and strictly without gold and silver, living frugally but with all their material needs provided for by the rest of the citizens. In such a way they will not become tyrants seeking to get the best of everything for themselves.

NOTES AND GLOSSARY:

life after death: (386c) spoken by the spirit of Achilles, hero of Homer's *Iliad* in Hades (the world of the dead) to Odysseus who is still living. It is particularly potent because in life Achilles had chosen a short life with fame in preference to a long life without distinction

the kingdom of the dead: (386d) from the battle of the gods at *Iliad*, XX, 64. In Homer the kingdom of the dead is a horrid place feared by men and gods alike

the mind after death: (386d) there is survival, but essential reality for Homer is earthly life. The two quotations are from *Iliad*, XXIII, 103 and *Odyssey*, X, 495 where the subject is Tiresias the blind prophet

the moment of death: (386d) the departure of the soul of Patroclus, friend of Achilles, killed by Hector in *Iliad*, XVI, 856

the spirit like smoke or bats: the disembodied spirit has lost all that makes him essentially human. In the first quotation (387a) the spirit is that of Patroclus who appears to Achilles requesting burial. Compare Plato's ideas and images of life after death in the myth of Er at the end of Book Ten

rivers of wailing and gloom: (387b) Acheron and Cocytus, rivers in Hades whose names suggest lamentation and wailing

Achilles's extravagant grief: (388a) over the death of his friend Patroclus, at *Iliad*, XXIV, 10 and XVIII, 23. Achilles is son of the goddess Thetis

Priam grovels: (388b) imploring the Trojans to let him go alone to Achilles to recover the corpse of his son Hector, *Iliad*, XXII, 414. Priam is king of Troy which is being besieged by the Greeks

Thetis grieves at her lot: (388b) *Iliad*, XVIII, 54

Zeus pities Hector: (388c) *Iliad*, XVII, 168. He also weeps for the impending death of his son Sarpendon and wishes that he could alter fate to save him (*Iliad*, XVI, 433)

the laughter of the gods: (389) Hephaestus is lame, a comic figure when acting as cupbearer to the gods at *Iliad*, I, 599

Diomedes's rebuke: (389e) to Sthenelus, his squire, who has just been arguing with Agamemnon, leader of the Greeks at Troy (*Iliad*, IV, 412)

the Achaeans: (389e) one of Homer's words for Greeks (*Iliad*, III, 8 and IV, 431)

Achilles insults Agamemnon: (389e) in the quarrel at the opening of the *Iliad* the insults are reciprocated (*Iliad*, I, 255)

Odysseus on food and drink: (390b) Odysseus is wise, in the sense of worldly wise, in Homer. Like all Homer's heroes he enjoys physical pleasures of the world, one of the greatest of which is the feast (*Odyssey*, IX, 8)

death by starvation: (390b) a sentiment not likely to encourage fortitude (*Odyssey*, XII, 342)

Zeus makes love to Hera: (390c) the story is told at *Iliad*, XIV, 294. Hera is his wife

Ares and Aphrodite: (390c) the god of war and the goddess of love. Aphrodite is the wife of Hephaestus, god of fire and craftsmanship. When he caught his wife in adultery with Ares he threw a net over the pair and all the gods laughed at their plight (*Odyssey*, VIII, 266)

Odysseus: (390d) a much enduring hero (*Odyssey*, XX, 17)

gifts sway the gods: (390e) in the Homeric world gifts were valued not only for their own sake but for the honour they brought the receiver (*Iliad*, IX, 515, and XIX, 278)

Achilles rebukes Apollo: (391) Apollo, god of the sun and music, supports Troy and lures Achilles away from the Trojans by taking the form of a Trojan noble whom Achilles pursues all over the Trojan plain (*Iliad*, XXII, 15, 20)

Scamander: (391b) the river that flows through the Trojan plain

Spercheius: (391b) a river near the birthplace of Achilles in northern Greece. He dedicated his lock to the river for his safe return (*Iliad*, XXI, 130, XXIII, 140)

Achilles and Hector: in the *Iliad* Achilles, having quarrelled with Agamemnon, withdraws from the fighting. When subsequently the Greeks are losing, Achilles allows his friend Patroclus to fight in his place. He is killed by Hector. Achilles, maddened by grief and despair, kills Hector and refuses to give up his body for burial, dragging it behind his chariot. He sacrifices eight young Trojan captives on the funeral pyre of Patroclus (*Iliad*, XXIV, 14; XXIII, 175)

Chiron: (391c) a wise centaur, half-man and half-horse, who educated a number of heroes including Achilles

Theseus and Peirithous: (391c) heroes who attempted to abduct Persephone, queen of the underworld

Ida: (391e) probably Mount Ida on Crete where Zeus spent his early years

representation in art: Plato's word is *mimesis*

beginning of the *Iliad*: (392e) Chryses is priest of Apollo. The god sends a plague to infest the Greek camp because Agamemnon is dishonouring his priest (*Iliad*, I, 15)

Ithaca: (393b) the island home of Odysseus, off north-west Greece

Argos: (393e) Agamemnon's home in the Peloponnese, just south of the isthmus of Corinth which joins north and south Greece

reciters: (395b) rhapsodes, professional performers who recited poetry (especially that of Homer) at festivals

myrrh and fillets of wool: (398a) the fillet is a headband. Traditional marks of honour. Plato honours poets, even though he banishes them from the ideal state

Ionian and Lydian styles: (398e) Ionia and Lydia are both in Asia Minor, well south of Troy. These are the more complicated styles of music

Dorian and Phrygian: (399a) Phrygia is a region around Troy. Dorian music, like Dorian architecture, was the severest style of all associated with archaic Greece and Sparta

Marsyas: (399e) he played the flute, Apollo the lyre: having challenged Apollo to a contest and lost, he was punished by death

Damon: (400b) a famous musician of the fifth century

Asclepius: (405e) son of Apollo, god of healing

Eurypylus wounded: (405e) at *Iliad*, XI, 583. The drink is given not to him but to Machaon and Nestor shortly afterwards

Herodicus: (406) a Thracian physician of the fifth century, tutor of Hippocrates, the famous Greek medical authority

Phocylides: (407) a sixth-century lyric poet

Midas: (408b) king of Phrygia: everything he touched turned to gold

the splendid myth: (414c) the phrase in Greek is often translated 'noble lie'; *pseudos* can mean lie or fiction. Note that the

guardians too are to be persuaded of the truth of
this story

Book Four

Adeimantus objects that the life prescribed for the guardians will not
be a happy one. Socrates replies that while it would not be at all surprising if the guardians were in fact very happy indeed, in founding the
new state it was not intended to legislate for happiness of a particular
class but for the community as a whole, each class enjoying that degree
of happiness its nature permits. The guardians must see that there are
no extremes of riches or poverty so that there is no internal dissension
between rich and poor. They must not permit the state to grow too
large in order to preserve its unity. The principle of promotion and
demotion from one class to another on the basis of merit must be strictly
adhered to. Above all no changes are to be made in the educational system; it is here that disorder may most easily creep in unobserved, undermining morals and manners until the whole of public and private life is
affected. All minor matters of legislation can be left to the discretion of
the rulers. Decisions about religious rites and institutions will be
referred to the authority of the oracle at Delphi.

Now that the state has been founded, it is necessary to discover where
justice and injustice can be found within it. Granted that the state so
founded is perfect, it will have in it the four cardinal virtues of wisdom,
courage, temperance, and justice. Wisdom in the state is to be found in
the knowledge of the ruling class of guardians. Courage is to be found
in that part of the state which fights for its defence, the auxiliaries, and
is further defined as the preservation of convictions inculcated by education about what is truly to be feared. Temperance (or discipline) is a
matter of the restraint with which each class recognises its own role.
The auxiliaries and artisans accept the rule of the guardians, and the
guardians accept their role as rulers. Temperance, then, is to be found
in the overall harmony of the state. Finally justice is the principle upon
which the state was originally founded and which makes the overall
unity of the state possible, the principle of the division of labour by
which each man minds his own business and does his own job without
meddling in the affairs of others. This keeps the three classes distinct,
each fulfilling its proper function without encroaching upon the other
two. Injustice is the reverse state of affairs.

These arguments are now applied from the state to the individual.
Since the virtues of the state are those of the individuals who make it
up, we can expect to find in the individual three principles corresponding to the classes in the state. If a man who is thirsty nevertheless
refuses to drink, there are two contrary impulses active within him

which may be identified as appetite or desire and reason or calculation. A third part in the soul is the spirited or assertive element. These three elements, the rational, the spirited and the appetitive in the individual correspond to the guardians, the auxiliaries, and the artisans in the state. The wisdom of the individual resides in his reason, his courage in the spirited part, and temperance is the harmony of the three parts when reason governs with the consent of spirit and appetite. The justice of the soul arises when each part fulfils its own proper function without trespassing on those of the others; injustice is the opposite condition. Justice is therefore the health and harmony of the soul; injustice its disease and discord. Socrates has now given a definition of justice and asks whether it pays better than injustice. Glaucon says that this is self-evident. But Socrates wishes to offer a complementary view of the bad state and the bad character for comparative purposes.

NOTES AND GLOSSARY:

statues: (420c) they were painted in ancient Greece

the big thing: (423d) as in the proverb of Archilochus referred to in Book Two at 365c

the latest song: (424b) *Odyssey*, I, 351

the Hydra's head: (426e) the Hydra was a monster with many heads that grew two heads if one was cut off. Eventually the great hero Heracles killed the monster by burning the heads

the oracle at Delphi: (427b) Delphi in northern Greece was the site of the most famous oracle in the Greek world through which it was thought the god Apollo, god of prophecy, gave utterance which was then interpreted by his priest. The oracle was regularly consulted in Plato's time

the earth's centre: (427c) at the omphalos or navel of the world. An omphalos was also the boss or centrepiece of a shield

Thracians and Scythians: (435e) Thrace is in northern Greece; traditionally the Thracians were considered to be a warlike race. The Scythians is a general name covering the various nomadic tribes of northern Europe and Asia, beyond the Black Sea

Phoenicians and Egyptians: (436) the Phoenicians were among the first great traders and colonisers of the ancient world, and like the Egyptians were regarded with respect as founders of civilisations older than those of Greece

Odysseus beats his breast: (441b) *Odyssey*, XX, 17

definition of justice: (441e) this is not simply a question of the three parts of the soul minding their own business, but the more positive notion of each part fulfilling its proper role and function

Book Five

Socrates is interrupted by Adeimantus who wishes to hear more about the community of women and children briefly referred to earlier. On the basis that difference of sex relates merely to the physical function of begetting and bearing children Socrates argues that women and men should be able to perform the same duties in the state according to their natural ability though men will generally perform better than women. Women are to be trained and educated exactly like the men. Women who are philosophic will become guardians; those who are spirited will become auxiliaries. Male and female guardians must not be allowed to live together in the same household. All women should be common to all men, and children should be held in common to be brought up in state nurseries. No parent should know its own child; no child should know its own parent. Unions between guardians are to be regulated entirely by the state. There will be mating festivals at which rulers will arrange for the best men to mate with the best women by a rigged ballot to avoid dissent, with the object of ensuring that the best offspring result. The population level is to be kept stable. As a result of these arrangements, the conflict of interest between the family and the state will be eliminated. The state will be one large family and so have maximum unity.

Socrates then discusses the conduct of war. Children are to be taken on campaigns and initiated into the art of war early on. Civilised rules of conduct are laid down. There must be no stripping of corpses or refusal to allow burial of the enemy. War between Greeks is to be regarded as a kind of civil strife.

Glaucon, impatient of detail, interrupts to ask whether such a state, admittedly desirable, can ever be realised as a practical possibility. Socrates replies that this is a secondary question which does not affect the soundness of the method or the truth that results from it. The ideal is no less true because it may not be realised on earth. Socrates then argues that existing states would become like the ideal after one principal change, that is, if philosophers were to become kings, or if kings and rulers were to become philosophers. He then defines what he means by philosopher. The philosopher is the lover of learning and knowledge, but more than this he is a lover of truth. Devotees of the arts enjoy all kinds of beautiful things in sound colour or shape, but the true philosopher sees beyond the surface of things into the essential nature of beauty itself. The philosopher seeks knowledge of the unchanging forms of beauty, justice, and so on. Others who content themselves with the particularities of the phenomenal world, that is, with what we can perceive by our senses, do not have the true knowledge of the philosopher but have only belief or opinion based on the mutable appearance of things.

NOTES AND GLOSSARY:

women and children held in common: (449d) referred to briefly earlier at 423e

Fate: (451) Plato's word is *nemesis*, meaning divine retribution for mortal presumption

gymnasium: (452) the Greek word is *palaestra* in which men exercised naked

Cretans and Spartans: (452c) Crete, the oldest centre of culture in the Greek world. The Spartans were notably athletic. It is generally thought that Plato had Aristophanes in mind in the reference here to comedians. See his play *Ecclesiazusae* ('Women in the Assembly'). Women were generally excluded from public life in Athens as in the rest of Greece

Arion's dolphin: (453d) Arion was an ancient bard who lived about 700BC. According to legend he was rescued from Corinthian sailors who coveted his treasure by a dolphin, one of a number who had been charmed by his music, and carried away from the ship on its back

mating festivals: (459e) Plato's language here intentionally brings to mind the stockbreeder. All the provisions are for eugenic purposes

infanticide: (460c) not uncommon in the Greek world. It seems that it is envisaged here

tenth or seventh month: (461d) the festivals will last some time (possibly a month). Women will give birth at different times according to the moment of conception which could be at the beginning or end of the festival. These arrangements are to prevent incest between parent and child. Plato does not seem to be bothered about sexual relations between siblings

Olympic victor: (465d) in the Olympic games, the most prestigious in Greece, held every four years at Olympia, the main sanctuary of Zeus in Greece

the happiness of the guardians: (465e) the earlier reference is at 420a

the half is more than the whole: (466c) from Hesiod's *Works and Days*, 40

the soldier in war: (468) the Athenian soldier took an oath not to disgrace his sacred shield

Ajax the brave: (468d) he had the better of a duel with Hector in *Iliad*, VII, 311

rewards for the brave: (468d) the basis of the aristocratic society in Homer, *Iliad*, VIII, 162

men of gold: (469) they become spirits: Hesiod, *Works and Days*, 122

barbarians: (469c) the Greek word *barbaroi* simply means non-Greeks

burial of the enemy: (469e) customary in Greece from Homeric times

is the state practicable?: (471e) a crucial stage in the structure of the *Republic*

ideal pattern: (472c) *paradeigma*, paradigm

philosopher rulers: (473d) another crucial point in the argument

Glaucon's passion for young men: (474d) homosexuality is accepted as entirely natural in the Greek world

the Dionysia: (475d) the term was given to festivals at which plays were performed. They were performed at the theatre of Dionysus in Athens

the riddle: (479b) commentators give the puzzle as follows: a man who is not a man (a eunuch) throws a stone that is not a stone (a pumice-stone) at a bird which is not a bird (a bat) sitting on a twig that is not a twig (a reed)

Book Six

Such philosophers who alone have knowledge of reality, the eternal, immutable world, will obviously be guardians of the state. The true philosopher's pleasures are those of the mind; he has contempt for physical pleasures, scorns money and is high-minded, just, and civilised. He learns easily and retains what he has learned. He has a true sense of proportion. To this Adeimantus objects that in practice most philosophers are either useless or vicious. Socrates agrees but lays the blame on present social and political organisation which is a corrupting environment for the philosopher. To produce a different kind of character uninfluenced by what common opinion regards as desirable is extremely difficult. Furthermore, philosophy is given a bad name by those who set themselves up as educators like the sophists. The few philosophers who can withstand the corrupting influences around them withdraw from political life, content to live quietly away from the world. But if the world realises its error (and there is no reason why it should not), philosophy will take its rightful place at the centre of political life and then the ideal state will be possible. The proposals already laid down are the ideal, and to put them into effect will be difficult but not impossible.

Socrates resumes discussion of the education of the guardians on the principle that the guardians must be philosophers. There must be a series of intellectual studies to test the individual to see whether he or she has the ability to pursue the highest forms of knowledge, leading ultimately to knowledge of the good. Most think that pleasure is the chief good, while the more refined think that it is knowledge. But Socrates insists that there is no value in knowledge unless it leads us to know the good from which all things derive their purpose and value. The good is something that every soul pursues, the motive of all its actions. It is difficult fully to comprehend. When pressed to define the good in specific terms Socrates confesses that he is unable to do so, and proceeds by analogy. In the phenomenal world that is recognised by the senses, there are the sun, the eye, and visible objects; corresponding to which in the intelligible world there are the good, the intelligence or reason, and the immutable and eternal forms of things. The good illuminates all, making the world intelligible as the sun makes it visible, and is the cause of all that exists. From the simile of the sun, Socrates proceeds to the analogy of the divided line to show the relationship between the visible and the intelligible worlds. Imagine a line divided into four parts; two belong to the visible and two belong to the intelligible world. In the different segments moving from obscurity to clarity are, first, the images and shadows of things, second, sensible and material objects themselves, third, in the intelligible sphere the abstractions of mathematics, and, fourth, the eternal and immutable forms of things. The four equivalent states of mind are first, imagining or perhaps illusion, second, belief, third, thinking or understanding, and fourth, intelligence or true knowledge.

NOTES AND GLOSSARY:

Momus:	(487) god of fault-finding and mockery
the epigram:	(489c) Simonides, when asked whether it was better to be rich or a genius, replied that it was better to be a rich man since men of genius were to be found at the court of the rich
the sophists:	(492) the common view is reflected in Aristophanes's comedy *The Clouds*. Plato argues that the sophists merely reflect public opinion and are products of the environment
fatal necessity:	(493d) Plato has 'the necessity of Diomedes' of uncertain reference. Diomedes is one of the heroes of Homer's *Iliad*

Theages: (496c) another proverb of uncertain derivation

Socrates's divine sign: (496c) an inner voice referred to at *Apology*, 31c

the true philosopher withdraws from the world: (496e) perhaps a reference to Plato himself

Heraclitus's sun: (498b) he believed that there is a new sun every day, as everything changes and is in a state of constant flux

life after death: (498c) the first reference in the dialogue

matched phrases: (498e) thought to refer to the practice of Isocrates (436–338BC), who taught the art of fine writing in a school that was a rival of Plato's Academy

qualities of the rulers: (503a) described at 413e

qualities of the philosophic character: described at 484–87b

the three parts of the mind: (504) the discussion begins at 484

the longer route: (504b) referred to at 435d

discussion of beautiful things and beauty itself: (507) begins at 476b

assumptions: (510b) translating the Greek *hypotheses*

the first principle: (511b) that is, the ground of all assumptions

---

Book Seven

Socrates clarifies what he has been saying by means of a third analogy using the allegory of the cave to illustrate the degrees in which human nature may be ignorant or enlightened. Imagine men chained from birth in a dark underground cave with their backs to the entrance of the cavern. Behind them is a fire and between the fire and the men a road on higher ground. Along this road men carry various articles the shadows of which will appear to the men in the cave to be the only realities because they cannot turn their heads. Suppose one of them is let loose and is first taken to the fire to see the objects which before he had seen only as shadows, and then is taken up to the light: he will need to grow accustomed to the light before he can see the new reality of life beyond the cave. The last thing he will be able to do is to gaze upon the sun. If he goes back to the darkness of the cave, he will again be blinded and make a fool of himself in the eyes of his fellow prisoners. This parable represents the progress towards enlightenment, culminating in knowledge of the good, the vision of the sun. It further shows that the purpose of education is not to implant knowledge that was not there before as if sight could be put into blind eyes, but to turn the whole soul round and enable the eye of the soul, reason or intelligence, to see what is truly real. The unenlightened who are inured to the prison of lower things can never govern properly. Philosophers will be required to go back into the world and share their knowledge with the unenlightened.

Socrates now describes the higher education necessary to produce the true philosopher, since the physical and literary education described earlier is designed to produce an harmonious and balanced character rather than arrive at true knowledge. This is to be brought about by studies which turn the mind from the material world of sense to the objects of pure thought. The philosopher ruler must study the various branches of mathematics such as arithmetic, plane and solid geometry, astronomy, and harmonics. These are to be studied not for any practical advantages they may bring but purely to exercise the mind in logical and dialectical skills. Then comes the final stage of study, dialectic, the exercise of pure thought that is not dependent upon the sensible world or hypotheses about the sensible world as is mathematics. Socrates says that it is not possible to define it, as fully to understand dialectic is to have knowledge. It is concerned with first principles until ultimately it results in an apprehension of the good.

Socrates discusses the qualities of character and mind that will be necessary for the philosopher rulers, and then gives details of the ages at which they will begin each stage of their education. Literary and physical education lasts until the age of eighteen. The next two years are spent in military service. Ten years of mathematics follow between twenty and thirty. Those who do well will go on to five years of dialectic. Then follow fifteen years of practical experience in minor offices, after which those who are successful in all these practical and intellectual tests will be fully fledged philosopher rulers at the age of fifty.

NOTES AND GLOSSARY:

the released prisoner: (516d) would rather be 'a slave in the house of a landless man', words spoken by Achilles in Hades in *Odyssey*, XI, 489, implying that the cave is like Hades

the unenlightened will kill their saviour: (517) an allusion to the death of Socrates

the happiness of society as a whole: (519e) see similar statements at 420b and 466

king-bees: (520b) the Greeks thought that queen bees were male. This figure of the hive is made much of in the following book: see 552c, 559d, 564b, 573

eager rulers the worst: (520d) refers to the point made by Thrasymachus at 347b

spinning: (521c) a child's game involving the spinning of a shell, black on one side, white on the other. One child calls night or day, and is the chaser or chased depending on which side the shell comes to rest

Palamedes: (522d) a Greek sage. Plato's view is that knowledge of number was not the invention of a hero figure, but came naturally through experience of the world

plane geometry: (526c) geometry relating to one-dimensional flat surfaces as opposed to solid geometry that deals with multidimensional bodies

Daedalus: (529e) the legendary Cretan craftsman who built the labyrinth for King Minos of Crete

the Pythagoreans: (530d) this school of philosophy studied mathematics and music among other things

the torture of slaves: (531b)torture of slaves for the purpose of obtaining evidence was legal in Greece

terms: (532e) Plato is not concerned to develop a systematic technical language

irrational lines: (534d) a geometrical term

qualities of the rulers: (535c) described at 412b

unworthy philosophers: (535c) discussed at 495c

choice of elderly men: (536c) see 412c

Solon: (536d) an Athenian sage and legislator of the sixth century to whom many wise sayings were attributed

mathematics for the young: (536d) in addition to literature and music described earlier

cross examination: (539b) the method of Socrates himself

the islands of the blest: (540b) a traditional image of heaven

Pythian oracle: (540c) the oracle of Apollo at Delphi. Apollo slew the monstrous Python and so acquired the epithet Pythian

---

Book Eight

Having completed his account of the virtuous state, Socrates now takes up the argument where he had left it at the end of Book Four, and describes unjust states and injustice in the individual. Four main types are distinguished: timocracy, oligarchy, democracy, and tyranny. As the character of the state reflects the character of the individuals who make it up, there will be four corresponding classes of individuals inferior to the truly just and good man already described.

All human things are subject to decay and in the course of time in the perfect commonwealth there will be strife within the ruling class and then between classes. The reasons for such a decline cannot wholly be explained but the probable result will be a compromise between the guardians and the auxiliaries whereby they divide the property of the other citizens and enslave those whom they formerly guarded as freemen. In such a state the spirited element will be predominant, shown in overvaluation of the physical at the expense of the intellectual and in a general warlike and ambitious spirit. Socrates calls this state timocracy, the government of honour. In the timocratical individual the spirited element and the love of honour predominate but he is flawed because of the loss of the guiding influence of reason and philosophy. He may be regarded as the son of the aristocrat seduced by bad influence from following his father's example.

The love of wealth which came with timocracy grows until the state becomes an oligarchy in which the minority who own property have political power from which those who do not own property are excluded. The oligarchic man may be regarded as the son of the timocratical man whose love of honour has been diverted into the love of gain. He is hardworking and outwardly respectable but essentially driven by fear and subject to inner conflict, generated by the desire to make money and the need to maintain his position.

Those excluded from the wealth of the state rise up against the oligarchs and establish equality and equal rights for all, democracy. Liberty degenerates into licence and anarchy. The democratic man departs from the economy and restraint of his oligarchic father and becomes a prey to extravagant and unnecessary desires. He lives for pleasure from day to day, satisfying every appetite and whim without any ruling principle.

The excessive desire for liberty undermines democracy and by natural reaction sets the scene for tyranny. All respect for authority is overthrown and the state splits into factions. The largest faction, the impoverished masses, seek a leader in their battle against the wealthy oligarchs. This leader gradually becomes more powerful until before the people realise it he has acquired a bodyguard and effectively made them slaves.

NOTES AND GLOSSARY:

resuming the argument: (543c) from the opening of Book Five (449) where Socrates had been interrupted

Cretan and Spartan states: (544c) rule by a military élite. In Sparta the ruling class was greatly outnumbered by a subject population of Helots

the geometrical number: (546b and following) a difficult passage, thought by some to be not wholly serious

Hesiod's metals: (546e) in the *Theogony* Hesiod describes the Golden Age which gives way to the silver age which becomes the bronze age until it degenerates into the age of iron. Compare the myth of metals at 415

oligarchy: (550c) means rule by the few, who are also rich, so that Plato is here describing a plutocracy

cavalryman or infantryman: (552) these had to provide their own armour so that they were a professional class

the blind god: (554b) Plutus, god of wealth

appointment by lot: (557) in the Athenian democracy jurors and most magistrates were chosen by lot from the adult male population

Lotus-eaters: (560c) in the *Odyssey* the lotus is a drug which causes anyone who takes it to forget the world of business and responsibilities

assembly: (565b) the sovereign body of the Athenian democracy in which every male adult could vote and speak, possibly as many as 50,000 in all

Zeus Lykaeus in Arcadia: (565d) the worship of Zeus in Arcadia (in the central Peloponnese) was instituted according to legend by Lykaeus

Croesus: (566c) the rich king of Lydia whose story is told in Herodotus, *Histories*, 1, 55

the champion overthrown: (566d) Hector's charioteer at *Iliad*, XVI, 766

Euripides: (568) (*c*.485–406BC) famous tragic playwright whose plays show evidence of the influence of the sophist movement

Book Nine

Whereas in the democratic man all appetites have equal rights, his offspring the tyrannical man is dominated by one master passion which enslaves all the elements of the soul and ministers to the basest and most bestial appetites whose existence is revealed in dreams. There is no taboo he will not violate and no excess from which he will shrink. He is the perfect example of the unjust man.

Socrates ranks the states and individuals in order of happiness. The philosopher ruler and tyrant are opposite extremes in respect not only to justice but also to happiness. The tyrant enslaved by his own passions which he can never satisfy and fearful of those around him is neither free nor truly rich or happy.

It has been established that the soul of man is composed of three parts, the rational, the spirited and the appetitive, each of which has its own pleasure. The philosopher ruled by reason seeks knowledge, the spirited man seeks honour, and the man of appetite seeks fulfilment of appetite, often through riches. Which is the greatest pleasure? In the first place, only the philosopher has tasted the pleasures of all three parts and only the philosopher has developed in him the capacity for sound judgement based on knowledge. Only he can truly judge of pleasure: the pleasures of wisdom come first, those of honour second and those of appetite, such as riches, third. In the second place, since the philosopher alone is in contact with realities, he alone can know the essence of true pleasure. Other pleasures are to some extent illusory. True pleasure is only experienced when the soul is harmoniously ordered under the rule of reason, so that the more reasonable the desire, the greater is the pleasure in its gratification. In the third place, what is furthest removed from reason is also furthest from law and order, so that the tyrant is furthest from true pleasure (while the philosopher ruler is nearest). For these reasons it is possible to say that the life of the philosopher ruler will be infinitely more happy than that of the tyrant.

It is now possible to answer Thrasymachus's claim that injustice pays best if the injustice goes undetected or unpunished. Imagine the human soul represented by the figure of a man, a lion (the spirited element) and a many-headed monster (the appetitive element) combined into one form outwardly human. To argue that injustice pays is to say that it pays to let the monster have its own way and to feed the lion at the expense of the man so that he becomes so weak that the other two parts can completely control him. In conclusion, all ought to be ordered and controlled by justice, preferably coming from within or, failing that, imposed from without. Even if the ideal state cannot be realised on earth, the philosopher can so order his life that he finds the pattern of it in himself.

NOTES AND GLOSSARY:

unnecessary pleasures: (571b) described at 558d

living with a tyrant: (577b) it is generally thought that Plato writes with his own experience in mind; in 388/7 he had visited Sicily and lived with Dionysius I of Syracuse

the phantom Helen: (586c) In Greek myth, Helen was the cause of the Trojan war when the Trojan Paris abducted her from Sparta where she was wife of Menelaus, brother of Agamemnon. Paris had been asked to judge which of the three senior goddesses (Hera, Athene and Aphrodite) was the fairest. Aphrodite, the goddess of love, offered him Helen, the most beautiful woman in the world, if he chose her. In his play *Helen* Euripides makes Hera substitute a phantom figure for the real Helen. The story occurs in Stesichorus, a lyric poet of the early sixth century

the pleasures of the soul: (587) each element will have its own, so that Plato does not envisage mortification of the flesh

the computation of happiness: (587b) it is generally thought that there is humour in this passage

injustice pays: (588b) the original argument at 361

Chimaera, Scylla and Cerberus: (588c) famous monsters in Greek mythology. Chimaera had three heads and was part-lion part-dragon and part-goat. Scylla was a woman above the waist; her lower part was changed into the tail of a serpent surrounded by dogs. Cerberus was the three-headed dog who guarded the entrance to the underworld

Eriphyle: (590) bribed by Polynices with a necklace to persuade her husband to join the expedition of the Seven against Thebes to restore Polynices to his throne in place of his brother Eteocles

government for the good of the subject: (590d) not as Thrasymachus had argued at 343−4

Book Ten

Socrates returns to the subject of poetry first treated in Book Two, and asks what relation artistic representation has to truth. Take, for example, a bed or table. There is the form or archetype of the bed made by god, an actual bed made by the carpenter and a representation of the bed made by the painter which is a copy of the actual bed which in turn is a copy of the form of the bed. The poet is in the same relation to reality as the painter of the bed, that is, he produces a copy of a copy; he is at two removes from true reality, the world of forms, imitating merely the mutable phenomenal world of sense impression, the world of common opinion and belief.

Again it may be said that there are three arts concerned with any object; the art of using it, the art of making it, and the art of representing it. Only the user has the knowledge of the object and instructs the maker how to make it; the maker therefore has correct opinion. The representational artist on the other hand has neither true knowledge nor correct opinion but only imprecise third-hand impressions about what he is imitating. Furthermore, poetry appeals not to the highest part of our nature, the rational part of the soul, but to the emotions and the inferior parts of the soul. It therefore wakens and stimulates the lower elements at the expense of controlling reason. Finally poetry can corrupt even the best characters by making us sympathise and identify with the sufferings of others, undermining our capacity to endure our own troubles. Only hymns to the gods and eulogies of good men should be allowed in the state; if other forms are admitted, pleasure and pain will rule in the place of law and reason.

Socrates goes on to describe the rewards that goodness can win, which leads him to argue for the immortality of the soul and consider the life after death. As everything has its own particular good so it has its own particular evil through which it may be destroyed as illness may destroy the body. But injustice and moral infirmity cannot destroy the soul which is therefore immortal. Virtue is its own reward, and this has been proved in the course of the argument. Nevertheless virtue is rewarded in this life and in the next. The rewards in this life are as nothing compared with what awaits the just man after death. Socrates then relates the myth of Er, a man allowed to return to life after he had seen the judgement of souls and the punishment of the wicked after death. He tells of a cycle of reincarnation which is a penalty for former sins, and of the structure of the universe which hinges upon the spindle of necessity turned by the fates. He sees the souls choosing various patterns of life and drinking the waters of forgetfulness before reincarnation in mortal form. This tale must inspire us to keep to the upward way and in all things to seek justice with the help of wisdom.

NOTES AND GLOSSARY:

the form of bed: (597) compare 507b

the authority of Homer: (599c) claims were made that Homer was a master of all the technical arts which he had described in his poetry

Thales and Anacharsis: (600b) two of the seven sages of Greece flourishing in the seventh century. Thales was a philosopher but made himself rich from oil mills. Anacharsis is said to have invented the anchor and the potter's wheel

Pythagoreans: (600b) followers of Pythagoras, born in the sixth century on the island of Samos. One of the early philosophers of Greece, he is associated with the doctrine of the soul's immortality, a belief in reincarnation and the study of number. He held that the soul could be purified, especially by study

Creophylus: (600b) an epic poet from Chios, an island in the eastern Aegean

Protagoras and Prodicus: (600c) two of the most famous sophists of the late fifth century

conflicts: (603d) see also 439c

endurance of ill fortune: (603e) the subject of 387d

the quarrel between poetry and philosopy: (607b) the earliest philosophers of the sixth century, like Xemophanes and Heraclitus, had criticised Homer's conception and presentation of the gods. Hence developed the allegorical interpretation of Homer

justice and rewards: (612b) see 363a

Gyges's ring: (612b) see 359d

the gods, the just and the unjust: (612e) see 352b

the unjust man: (613c) see 362

Odysseus's tale to Alcinous: (614b) told over four books in the *Odyssey*
and proverbially a long tale. It includes Homer's
account of the underworld which Plato regarded as
false

Pamphylia: (614b) in Asia Minor

Tartarus: (616) traditionally a place of eternal punishment

trireme: (616c) a Greek ship with three ranks of oars on
each side

Orpheus: (620) the mythical bard was torn to pieces by Mae-
nads, women possessed by the god Dionysus

Thamyris: (620) he was deprived of his sight and his power of
song after challenging the Muses to a contest

Ajax: (620b) Ajax and Odysseus quarrelled over the divine
armour of Achilles after his death. The Greeks
awarded it to Odysseus. Ajax was maddened to the
extent of committing suicide

Agamemnon: (620b) king of men, he chose to be an eagle, king of
birds. He was murdered by his wife Clytemnestra
on his return from Troy

Atalanta: (620b) a famous runner from Calydon in Arcadia.
Only a man who could defeat her in a foot-race
could marry her. Hippomenes did so by distracting
her with golden apples

Epeius: (620c) he made the wooden horse by means of
which Troy was taken

Thersites: (620c) a common soldier who insulted Agamemnon
and Odysseus in a council in the *Iliad*

Odysseus: (620c) his ten-year wanderings from Troy to Ithaca
are recounted in the *Odyssey*

Lethe: (621a) the river of forgetfulness

Part 3

Commentary

The dialogue form

The dialogue form in which the *Republic* is written is a distinctive feature of all Plato's writings and has come to be particularly associated with him. In all but one or two of his later works the leading character who conducts the dialogue is Socrates, so that Plato's dialogues are sometimes called Socratic dialogues. For these dialogues Plato goes to the trouble of creating characters and a setting in which there is the illusion of spontaneous discussion (498e). In fact he treats his dialogues in the same way as a playwright or a novelist treats his fictional creations. This is not at all what might be expected of a philosopher. Most philosophy is, after all, cast in quite a different mould. Philosophers before Plato habitually wrote didactic treatises, often in verse, wrapping up their conclusions in gnomic utterances that represented the results of their thought crystallised in memorable form. After Plato philosophy has tended to be a systematic and formal treatment of topics arranged according to some set scheme and written in a detached impersonal third-person style, using technical language and assuming some acquaintance with the subject. To ask why Plato chose to use the dialogue form, and, within the dialogue, to re-create the character of Socrates long after the historical Socrates had died is to ask fundamental questions about Plato's philosophical method.

In creating the Socratic dialogue, Plato is affirming the soundness of Socrates's methods and the moral seriousness of his mission as an educator of mankind and midwife to truth (as described in the Introduction, page 10 above). In his life, his mission, and his death Socrates embodied for Plato the true philosophic spirit. The Platonic Socrates of the dialogues is an imaginative extension of this spirit. In his spiritual and intellectual integrity manifested in his method of discourse, in his appeal to and application of reason and in his moral insight, Plato's Socrates is wholly superior to those whose arguments he refutes such as the sophist Thrasymachus in Book One of the *Republic*. He is therefore a model, a representation in action of the kind of man who believes that virtue is knowledge. The dialogues are therefore exemplary and show how the philosophic spirit is to be used as a force for enlightenment as envisaged in the allegory of the cave (514–17) and in the myth of Er (618c)

The Socratic method further dramatises the very nature of thinking itself. In the *Theaetetus* Plato describes the process of thinking as the discourse that the mind carries on with itself about any subject it is considering. 'I have a notion that when the mind is thinking it is simply talking to itself asking questions and answering and saying yes or no' (*Theaetetus*, 189c). All thinking is therefore dialogue, whether the dialogue be conducted with others or within the mind itself. And so Plato always begins at the beginning with a simple question; nothing is presumed. The question is then examined, the assumptions behind it may be questioned, conventional views of the matter are dismissed, perhaps the question is redefined or shown not to be the real question at issue at all. From the initial opening the argument may take many unpredictable turns that result in surprising conclusions or a conclusion in which nothing is concluded. Such is the character of Plato's dialogues in which the mind is brought up against other arguments to which it must respond and in the course of which it may be sidetracked into considering all kinds of objections relevant or irrelevant before clarity can be reached upon the issue at hand. Accordingly, what we have in Plato's dialogues is not the communication of a fully developed philosophical system, however influential 'Platonism' has been. There is evidence, assuming that Plato is indeed the author of the letters attributed to him (there is some dispute about this among scholars) that Plato deliberately refrained from committing much of his more advanced thought to paper. Interesting here is the testimony of Aristotle who records that those who came to hear Plato talking about the Good in the Academy were surprised to hear nothing but mathematics, astronomy, and the limit of the One. Of this there is little in Plato's dialogues which appear to have been designed for popular consumption, not as 'popular philosophy' but as a demonstration both of the spirit in which philosophy is to be conducted and of the ends which it is to serve. What we have in the Socratic dialogues is Plato's dramatisation of the pursuit of truth.

And so the *Republic* starts naturalistically like a novel with a realistic setting, not described in as much detail as that of some of the other dialogues, but with enough to suggest the connection of Socrates and his enquiries with everyday life. Socrates and his friends have been to a festival, enjoyed a procession and said the prayers for which they had gone in the first place (Socrates is no atheist), when they meet Polemarchus, who takes them to the house of his old father Cephalus. The opening is written very much in the familiar style, in what the Greeks called *lexis eiromene*, in speech as it is spoken. The conversaton with Cephalus on the subject of old age leads naturally to the question of the good life and to the fundamental question of the dialogue: what is justice?, that is, what is right conduct or in an old-fashioned word, righteousness? The dialogue is, therefore, rooted in normal intelligent conversation between people of goodwill, for Cephalus, a friend of Socrates, is as eager to talk to Socrates as Socrates is to listen to him. What is true of the opening is true of the whole. The dialogue is designed to be intelligible to the general reader throughout. Only those parts where current mathematical or musical notions are being discussed present difficulties, and these difficulties are a result of our ignorance about current knowledge which Plato took for granted and shared with his educated audience, and are felt by specialists as much as by beginners. In the fictional dialogue Socrates is required to explain himself clearly to his respondents who represent a non-specialist audience. To that end he does not speak in technical language, and specifically refuses to argue over names or terms (533e) in even the most metaphysical parts of his enquiry.

Like characters in a novel all Plato's protagonists have their particular roles to play. Cephalus, though briefly drawn, emerges clearly as a representative figure who introduces conventional wisdom about morality and justice. A successful merchant who nevertheless does not believe that money is the be-all and end-all, Cephalus is decent and fair-minded, and speaks with the authority of experience. Polemarchus has inherited his father's decency and fair-mindedness but, without his experience, he appeals to the traditional authority of the poet. Socrates's cross-examination of his proposition that justice consists in giving every man his due constitutes the first demonstration of Socratic irony leading to refutation. Thereupon comes the most dramatic confrontation of the introduction and indeed of the whole dialogue with the interruption of Thrasymachus the sophist.

After the polite and careful cross-questioning of the sweetly reasonable Socrates the abrupt denunciation of him by Thrasymachus comes as a startling surprise. Plato has deliberately accentuated the contrast between Socrates and Thrasymachus for dramatic effect and has been accused of caricaturing the sophists in the process. Far from being sweetly reasonable, Thrasymachus is rude, impatient, opinionated and assertive. Soon after his intervention he announces that if he is to give his views it will be for a fee (337d). One of the many ways in which Socrates is to be distinguished from the sophists is his refusal to accept payment even when his services are requested, let alone when involved in a spontaneous discussion as is Thrasymachus here. The request for a fee immediately contaminates him in the reader's eye; this is not the conduct of one whose pursuit of truth is wholly disinterested. When Thrasymachus speaks, it is to give first a series of dogmatic assertions and then a lengthy and vigorous harangue which Socrates calls a 'flood of speech' (344d). So uninterested in argument is Thrasymachus that after he has asserted his view that justice is the interest of the stronger and that self-interest is what does and should motivate the wise man, he is ready to depart (344d). The others insist that he stay and answer his case. Socrates recognises that it is open to him to make a set speech like Thrasymachus in favour of justice in the form of a debating speech designed to appeal to a jury, but rejects this in favour of his usual method of proceeding by mutually agreed admissions (348b). By this method he gradually demonstrates the inadequacy of the views of Thrasymachus who is no match for Socrates in argument. But the contrast between Socrates and the sophist is not so completely one-sided. Thrasymachus is allowed fair insight into and criticism of Socrates's method. Thrasymachus points out the negative effect of Socratic irony and accuses him of shamming ignorance and never giving his own views (336c, 337a, e). He further caricatures the Socratic dialogue in a way that must raise a smile in every reader of Plato who has ever been impatient of the readiness with which Socrates's respondents answer yes or no (350d, e). It is a mark of Plato's humanity that he is able to turn his irony against himself. Socrates and Thrasymachus are diametrically opposed, therefore, not only in viewpoint and character but also in their methods. Plato's portrayal of Thrasymachus is deliberately extreme; the contrasting example of the sophist throws the superior qualities of Socrates's mind, motive, and method into clear relief.

The two remaining characters to be considered are Glaucon and Adeimantus, who are the main respondents after Book One. They have the simple function of setting the dialogue in motion and responding to the argument of Socrates. After he has disposed of Thrasymachus's argument and reduced him to silence, Socrates confesses that the discussion has been negative, since no positive definition of justice has been advanced; they have been deflected from their original question (354b). The first book ends like many of the earlier dialogues of Plato in an admission of ignorance, in perplexity or impasse (the Greek word is *aporia*). Glaucon and Adeimantus then re-state the main lines of Thrasymachus's argument and challenge Socrates to show that justice is desirable for itself. They are not hardened in their opinions in the way that Thrasymachus is at the outset, nor do they share his cynical view of life. Glaucon specifically says that he believes all that Socrates has to say about justice but cannot answer Thrasymachus's argument (358c). It is not clear how these two young men spend their time but they are not professional teachers like Thrasymachus, and indeed they are not at all practised in philosophical discourse. At one point Glaucon confesses that all he can do is to follow Socrates's lead and understand what is pointed out to him (432c). Nevertheless they are intelligent and have a natural interest in discovering the best kind of life from whatever source (365). They may be said therefore to represent not only the kind of people with whom the historical Socrates enjoyed conversation but also the ideal audience for which Plato wrote his dialogues. Despite their lack of any specialist knowledge, together with a quick mental grasp they have the principal qualification needed for the understanding of Plato's thought, an eager and disinterested desire for truth. They are ideal candidates for enlightenment and the constructive argument of the *Republic* is put into motion by their questioning.

We may believe that the Socratic dialogues as we have them represent Plato's thought in a popular form and suspect that his methods in the Academy itself may have been rather different. But if his teaching in the Academy was pitched at a higher level, it is unlikely to have been radically different in method, given that the culmination of the education prescribed for the philosopher rulers in the *Republic* is five years of dialectic. Socrates does not specifically define the term but it is clear from what he says that as the word itself suggests it is a developed form of the reasoning that Socrates demonsrates in the *Republic*.

The organisation of the argument

Although Plato creates the illusion of a free spontaneous discussion, the *Republic* is of course an organised discourse in which Plato seeks to enlighten his audience with particular ends in view. The dialogue form in which there is an imitation of a natural discussion precludes any schematic treatment whereby careful distinctions are maintained between the various branches of philosophy relating to metaphysics, ethics, politics and psychology. The *Republic* is remarkable because it includes so much and attempts a total view of human life as it is and as it might be.

Although the enquiry takes us in many directions there is nevertheless an overall unity of subject in the *Republic*. That subject is of course suggested in the second title given to the work by the ancients, 'Concerning justice'. Gradually in the course of the preliminaries Socrates is required to refute the argument that injustice pays by showing that justice is intrinsically valuable for its own sake. Thereafter the constructive argument of the *Republic* proceeds step by step as one thing leads naturally and logically to another. That is to say, Socrates and his respondents agree to begin with the origin of justice in society on the principle that justice can more easily be seen writ large in the state than in the individual. Socrates describes first the growth of the primitive state, arising from the fact of mutual need and based on the principle of the division of labour and then proceeds to the development of the civilised state, springing from the desire for luxury, the consequences of which are war and the need for a guardian class of soldiers to defend the state. If they are to do their job without harm to the state, these guardians must be properly trained in the right education. Imperceptibly the argument passes into prescriptions for the ideal state, for the making of good guardians. Socrates further outlines what will be the best form of society, given the requirements of human nature. Because the society envisaged is ideal it will necessarily be a just state and it will be possible to define what justice is in the state. The argument is then applied to the individual. But the definition produced by Socrates is only a stage in the argument of the *Republic*, not its climax; the argument leading up to the definition provokes questions which are asked by Socrates's respondents in Book Five and Socrates proceeds to a fuller and deeper definition of what constitutes a good guardian or philosophic ruler in which the basic principles and groundwork of the whole argument are gradually and specifically revealed. The good guardian is the true philosopher who has knowledge of the good. Socrates then contrasts justice in the ideal state and the true philosopher with various forms of injustice, leading to the comparison of the philosopher ruler with the tyrant in which the argument of Thrasymachus is finally overthrown. Leaving aside for the moment the question of the final book, it is apparent that in all its twists and turns the argument is directed towards one end which is held in view from the beginning.

It is one thing to be convinced of the overall unity of subject matter in the *Republic*, and quite another to see why the argument proceeds on the particular lines that it does. The modern reader will not expect that an enquiry into justice or morality will necessarily lead so quickly into the construction of an ideal state, and find the method of arguing from the state to the individual, which is so readily agreed to by the participants in the dialogue (368e) and which is maintained throughout, altogether puzzling.

To a large extent, like Glaucon and Adeimantus we must simply accept Socrates's method of proceeding for the sake of the argument. But we may legitimately enquire why they should not have found the proceeding strange. The basic reason probably lies in the close practical identification and bond between the individual and his community in ordinary Greek life. Although the distinction between nature (*physis*) and law or convention (*nomos*) was already an old one by the time of Plato, it never occurred to any Greek thinker, as it might to the modern mind, to see the state as an institution that is essentially inimical to the individual's well-being. In the *Republic* the state is a natural growth coming into existence to satisfy mutual needs because no man is self-sufficient. The two principal ways in which man is seen to differ from the animal world involve his reasoning power (man is a rational animal) and his political organisation (man is a political animal). In the latter proposition man is political because he lives in a *polis* (a city state). In early Greek thought a man is therefore distinctively human by virtue of his developed political organisation.

This city state is not to be thought of as entirely analogous to the modern nation state. Ancient Greece comprised a multitude of small autonomous states the size of Athens and smaller. The city state included not only the city but also the surrounding countryside, Attica in the case of Athens. The population of classical Athens is estimated to have been about two hundred and fifty thousand. This is the closely knit social unit in which Plato lived and for which he was legislating in the *Republic*.

Plato starts with the community and proceeds to the individual on the declared basis that the life of the state is the life of the men composing it writ large in simple form and easy to see (368e). If the life of the state is the life of its individual members, then the converse applies, that the life of the individual will reflect the character of the state in which he grows up and lives. In legislating for an ideal state Plato is seeking to create the best conditions in which the virtue of the individual can flourish. Socrates fully recognises that the ideal state is a pattern laid up in heaven which anyone can see and establish in himself (592b). At the same time without the ideal environment he clearly fears that the individual effort will be faced with the greatest difficulties. This is apparent in his account of the position of the philosopher in the unreformed society (487b – 497). All his educational reforms are designed to protect the growing mind and soul from contamination from without. What he insists upon throughout the argument of the *Republic* is the natural and inevitable interplay between the state and the individual, or between the individual and his surrounding environment.

This natural and inevitable interrelationship is fundamental throughout, though it is not always presented naturalistically. That is to say, Plato does not describe social institutions in their rise and fall and their changing state in the manner of a historian. When he locates the origin of the state in mutual need arising from individual self-insufficiency, he represents the elementary form of the state as one in which only necessities are provided for (369 – 72). This is a logical account of the beginnings of social organisation rather than a historical one, and its purpose is to clarify the most elementary form of society satisfying basic human need. Similarly the gradual degeneration of the ideal state through timocracy, oligarchy and democracy to tyranny is a logical progression which is designed to clarify not an actual historical process but a psychological decline in which the lower elements of the psyche gradually come to dominate and are reflected in the institutions of the state. It is deliberately schematic for the sake of clarity. Plato wants us to be clear about different forms of injustice. But we are not to suppose that he believed that the progression might be historical or that all members of his oligarchic state have the characteristics of the oligarchic man; indeed the very nature of an oligarchy is the rule of the few. The correlation is general and logical rather than actual.

Once Plato's method of arguing from the state to the individual has been accepted, there are no major pitfalls for the modern reader. Indeed in his plan Plato has deliberately tried to take the reader along with him at every stage. A notable feature of the organisation of the *Republic* is the gradual unfolding of the thought in a series of readily graspable stages. In each stage the principles upon which the argument is proceeding are established and agreed in the course of discussion, so that it is always possible to know why a given topic is being treated at a particular stage. For example, Socrates establishes the principle that if the guardians are to do their job without harm to themselves and to the state, they must have an education in which their natural spirit and aggression are to be tempered by the cultivation of a philosophic disposition. This leads naturally into the first stage of the guardians' education. This is an adaptation of existing patterns of Hellenic education comprising the two elements of *mousike* (literature, the arts and all that comes within the domain of the Muses) and *gymnastike*, (physical education). Together these produce the Greek ideal of the all-round individual who has a balance of excellences intellectual, aesthetic, moral and physical. Plato's reform is designed to retain this balance while ensuring that everything taught is morally edifying. Only literature and music that encourage moral excellence are to be allowed in order to avoid the contamination of the growing soul by images of moral deformity. The whole discussion is governed by moral principles summed up at 400c–403e and is designed to answer the requirement set out at the beginning that a philosophic temperament is to be fostered in the guardians. When later Socrates comes to discuss the education of his philosopher rulers in Book Six, the discussion is conducted on a quite different basis. At this point we hear of an educational stage beyond that already described and of which there had been little hint previously. The education in mathematics and dialectic is to lead to knowledge of ultimate reality, the good itself. The basis of the whole discussion is the account of knowledge that has just been elucidated in Books Five and Six. This account of education is required by the statement about true knowledge which was itself required by the need to define the nature of the true philosopher. Plato has therefore split up his discussion of education into two separate accounts in order to suit the requirements of a gradually and naturally developing argument. It is only at the conclusion of the education of the philosopher that we see the whole pattern of Plato's education and what Plato has had in mind and been working towards from the beginning.

At this point it will be useful to distinguish five main divisions, or stages, in the argument. The division of the *Republic* into ten books of equal length is probably the result of ancient book production rather than the design of Plato himself, since the end of each book does not necessarily mark an obvious stage in the argument. This is notably true of the ends of Books Two and Eight. The five natural divisions are:

(1) Book One and part of Book Two (327–67). The first stage is concerned with the preliminary question, what is justice? The argument that injustice pays better and that the unjust man is happier than the just man is strongly put, and Socrates is required to show that justice is intrinsically desirable.

(2) The remainder of Book Two, and Books Three and Four (368–449). The second stage puts forward the positive statement of justice given by Socrates who previously had merely shown the inadequacy of conventional views. This involves the construction of the ideal state, the education necessary for its rulers and the argument from the state to the individual.

(3) Books Five, Six and Seven (449–541). The third stage takes the form of a digression when Socrates who is about to describe unjust states in order to contrast them with the ideal is interrupted, first, to explain more about the community of women and children, and, second, to say whether the ideal state can exist (471e). Arguing that if rulers become philosophers, the ideal state will come into existence, Socrates defines the nature of the true philosopher and lays down an educational programme to produce him.

(4) Books Eight and Nine (543–92). In the fourth stage Socrates picks up the argument where he had left it before being interrupted and proceeds to describe four unjust states (timocracy, oligarchy, democracy and tyranny), and four corresponding individual types which are to be contrasted with the ideal state and the just man. The argument that injustice pays and brings happiness is thoroughly refuted.

(5) Book Ten (595–621). In the final stage Socrates returns to the subject of poetry, indicating the superior authority of philosophy as a discipline of truth. He goes on to describe the rewards that justice can win which leads him to argue for the immortality of the soul and to relate the myth of Er.

The argument is seemingly continuous until the double interruption of Socrates between the second and third stages. With the definition of justice at the end of Book Four, Plato marks this climax in his argument with a climbing metaphor. Socrates says that they have climbed the top of a mountain in their argument from which they can see innumerable forms of vice and only one form of virtue (448c). He is about to enumerate these forms of wickedness when he is interrupted and asked to explain more about the community of women and children, briefly mentioned earlier (416d). There follows a long section on women and the arrangements to be made for children (449–71c). Strictly this is still part of the argument of the second stage. Why then did the description not come earlier at 416d? What is the point of the interruption? Plato has separated it for the purposes of clarity so that his reforms of existing education patterns are concentrated in one place. Socrates is then interrupted a second time and asked whether these reforms are practicable. This is a crucial question that will occur to the reader and there are advantages in facing it early on. But Plato could have contented himself with Socrates's general reply that the practicability of the proposals in no way affects the soundness of their enquiry without then going into the whole question of the philosophical state. Since nothing in the discussion of the unjust state in Books Eight and Nine depends on the metaphysical propositions of the intervening Books Five to Seven, his treatment of injustice in states and individuals could easily have come earlier, so that the philosophical state might have been the climax of the whole argument.

This, however, would clearly have been a most inferior plan for three principal reasons. In the first place, the third stage (Books Five to Seven), containing as it does the basic principles of Plato's thought, rightly comes nearer the centre of the work. In the second place, the whole movement of the argument would have been quite different were the fourth section to have preceded the third. In the plan which Plato has adopted, there is a steady and progressive upward movement from the investigation of the origin of justice in the primitive state which satisfies basic needs to the luxurious state which satisfies diverse appetites, to reform of this state ruled by guardians who are both spirited and philosophic, to the philosophic state where philosophers who know the good direct all the ends of human action. Thereafter comes the gradual decline from the ideal state to timocracy in which the spirited element is in the ascendancy, to the oligarchic state ruled by the appetite for money, to the democratic state ruled by diverse appetites for unnecessary pleasures, to tyranny in which all are enslaved to a dominant ruling passion. This rise and fall reveals a pattern of psychological growth and decline which gives a simple but clear direction to the argument. The postponement of Socrates's description of injustice is therefore vital to the good order of the work, since the continuous upward way of growth not only gives clarity and is aesthetically satisfying but also shows the possibility of the slow and gradual evolution in which man progresses from the natural life in which basic needs are satisfied to the fully philosophic state in which life is to be lived under the direction of reason in accordance with universal law. In the third place, although there is nothing in the description of the decline from the ideal state that depends upon the metaphysical propositions of the third section, in the comparison of the just with the unjust man that follows in Book Nine much of the argument is made more clinching by drawing on the theory of knowledge elucidated in the third section.

This leaves the fifth section on poetry and the immortality of the soul which some have considered to be an epilogue added afterwards to defend one of Plato's most controversial arguments; the attack on poetry. Whether or not this is true hardly affects the overall unity of subject in the work, since the attack on poetry is renewing a position already maintained earlier in the dialogue. But there remains the question why Plato did not put his attack on poetry all in one place. Is he not repeating himself, and therefore diminishing the concentration of his attack and spoiling the good order of his work? The answer to the first question is easy to see if we examine the contrasting arguments against poetry in the various sections in which they occur. In the beginning he finds poetry unsuitable for the education of the young on two principal grounds, theological and moral; it tells lies about the gods and it is morally unsound, showing heroes in a bad light and encouraging emotional excess in those who read it. In Book Ten he is able to force home the emotional and moral argument by making use of the tripartite division of the soul established at 435b, but in Book Ten the principal argument against poetry is that being a pale reflection of the world of sense impression it is at two removes from reality, the eternal immutable forms of things which Plato has described in Book Six. This argument (called the epistemological objection) can only come after Plato has introduced his theory of knowledge. Here Plato's constructive method is most easily demonstrated. The evolution of his argument is gradual and at no point in the argument does he ever take for granted any principle which has not been properly discussed and mutually understood by the participants in the dialogue and at no point does he anticipate views, principles or formulations that will not be established until later in the argument.

It still remains to ask why Plato delayed his epistemological attack upon poetry until Book Ten when he might have included it in the argument at any point after he had elucidated his theory of knowledge in Book Six. The answer must be that if he had included the attack in the section on the education necessary to bring the philosopher ruler to knowledge of reality, it would have been a negative distraction. The argument at this stage in Books Six and Seven is strongly forward-looking and positive. Furthermore, in a separate section in Book Ten, the attack acquires emphasis and prominence; it is not merely a negative sideline. This emphasis Plato desires because in attacking poetry he is attacking traditional and conventional wisdom in its most authoritative and potent form. He himself refers to the old battle between poetry and philosophy (607b) that had been going on since the earliest philosophers Xenophanes and Heraclitus attacked the view of the world in the poems of Homer and Hesiod. His purpose at the end of his dialogue is to offer a decisive blow in an old war. His audience might easily have been persuaded to reject the new wave of thinking associated with sophists like Thrasymachus, but the crucial reform for Plato is the reform of education which in his day was given over in large part to the study of poetry. Ultimately poetry is a greater enemy than Thrasymachus and his like.

It is not difficult to see why he ends the argument about the soul's immortality. The discussion begins with Socrates's desire to describe the rewards that goodness can win (608c). Although justice has been shown to be the health of the soul and therefore its own reward, an added incentive to virtue is the system of rewards and punishments described in the life after death graphically represented in the myth of Er. This will be discussed in the specimen essay, but, briefly stated, the final section in treating final things offers a persuasive conclusion in the solemn perspective put upon the argument by the prospect of death and judgement. All life is but a preparation for death in which the fate of the soul itself is at stake, so that we are well advised to keep our feet on the 'upward road' (621c). The dialogue opened with the physical journey to the Piraeus made for religious purposes. It ends with the description of the thousand-year journey of the soul. Between the two Plato has described the upward path upon which progress is to be made from the physical to the metaphysical and from earth to heaven.

In conclusion, Plato's method of argument in the *Republic* is not in a strictly rigorous sense either deductive or inductive. This is a necessary consequence of the dialogue form. That is to say, Plato does not start with a general proposition about justice and then deduce consequences from it. Nor is the positive definition of justice reached by considering individual examples of just behaviour from which a general definition can be induced. It is reached not by the inductive method, the origin of which Aristotle attributed to Socrates, but by a series of mutually agreed admissions (348b) about human life in society and in the individual from which consequences are deduced and further inferences induced. The argument proceeds by definite stages in each of which a principle is established and applied at the same time. The principles (or underlying propositions upon which the argument is based) are not enunciated at the beginning, nor do they represent the conclusion of the work; they are revealed according to need. This method of conducting an argument is called by philosophers 'constructive' or 'genetic'. A genetic definition is one that defines a thing by describing the manner of its formation, by describing it in the making, by describing it as becoming.

This definition suggests a fundamental truth about the Platonic dialogue in general and about the *Republic* in particular. Plato's dialogues are designed not so much to arrive at definitions as to show definitions in the making. In the *Republic* Socrates will not be drawn into attempting precise definitions of the form of the good or of the dialectic by which eventually it can be known. Once he has opened up the prospect before us, Socrates feels he has gone far enough, for the main point of his concern is to show justice in the making. Hence he starts with its origin and development in society (and by implied transfer in the individual) and hence the emphasis in the *Republic* on education, the 'one big thing' (423d) that the guardians must adhere to, and which occupies so much of his attention in the constructive part of the dialogue. In posing and answering the question, what is justice?, Plato wishes to show how it can come to be in the community and in the individual.

The illustration of the argument

It is something of a paradox that Plato, who all but banished poets from his ideal state, should himself be the most poetical of philosophers, noted throughout the ages, unlike his pupil Aristotle, for his imaginative presentation of ideas. Even when the argument of the dialogue is concerned with abstractions and formal definitions it is constantly enlivened by picturesque analogies and vivid images of illustration. These may be on a small scale when, for example, Socrates likens the guardians to watchdogs (375) or when he imagines the young growing up among images of moral deformity as feeding on poisons in a noxious meadow until gradually the contagion spreads throughout their souls (401c). But Plato habitually uses extended illustrations in each stage of his argument.

Towards the end of the first section, the argument about injustice is graphically represented in the story of Gyges and his ring (359d). Towards the end of the second stage, Socrates introduces the allegory of the metals (414c). In the state this is to ensure cohesion and unity; it also has the function of illustrating for the reader in graphic form the order of the state and the principles on which it must be maintained. In the third stage, the ignorant hostility shown to the philosopher in the unreformed state is dramatised in the story of the sea captain (488). The conventional wisdom of the sophists who feed the people just what they want is satirised in the illustration of the man in charge of a large and powerful animal who has learned to observe its reactions and made a science out of them (493). The main metaphysical ideas of the *Republic* are clarified in the simile likening the form of the good to the sun, in the figure of the divided line, and in the allegory of the cave (507–17). Underlying the whole account of the decline of the ideal state in the fourth stage is a chain of imagery that is first introduced when the philosopher rulers are likened to king-bees who must maintain the good order of the hive (520b). The drones become increasingly destructive

(552c, 559d, 564b–565c, 567e, 573, 574d). The argument of this section is also illustrated by the repeated motif of the son who reacts against his father (549c, 553, 558d, 571d). Here it might be suggested that Plato's whole philosophical argument is illustrated figuratively in the comparison of the individual to the state. The state is the concrete external form given to illustrate inner psychological states. That is to say, basic human need is objectified in the primitive state (369b), developed appetites find expression in the luxurious state (372c). The ideal state is an illustration writ large of the rule of reason in man. The four states in the fourth section illustrate various stages of decline from this ideal as the previous states had shown growth towards it. Finally at the end of the fourth stage comes the image of the human being as a composite beast; part-lion, part-many-headed beast in human form (588c). The image is used to clarify the argument against Thrasymachus. To follow his argument is to feed the beast (compare the picture of the sophists at 493). The *Republic* ends with the extended illustration of the future of the soul in the myth of Er (614).

These extended illustrations are not distractions; they all relate to major points of emphasis: the power of the argument for injustice, the overriding need to maintain the rule of the guardians in the ideal state, the brutishness of ignorance, the false claims of the sophists, the illusory nature of the phenomenal world and the true objects of real knowledge, and so on. In his discussion of poetry, it is apparent that Plato was profoundly convinced of the power of poetry (which he greatly feared) to impress itself upon the mind and affect the soul of man. In the *Republic* his images are designed to provide clinching illustrations of crucial points in his argument. Although we may regard the poetry of his prose as part of a persuasive intention to make philosophy palatable and entice the hearts and minds of the sceptical, Plato always exerts the kind of rigid control over his own poetic powers that he required of poets in his ideal state who are to write not with an eye to pleasure but in an austere style that will be useful (398ab). Much of the beauty of his style stems not so much from the invention of images as from the judgement with which he applies them.

Although he frowns upon the allegorical interpretation of existing poetry on the practical and sensible grounds that the primary meaning is the one that impresses itself on the mind, not the ulterior meaning that may be read into it afterwards (378d), the developed allegory is one of Plato's favourite literary devices. In Greek, *allegoria* basically means a description of one thing under the image of another. Whereas a simile may make only one point of comparison and contain within it many details that bear no relation to the basic point of the comparison, an allegory is a more controlled likeness in which there are many correspondences between the details of the image and the reality to which it is being compared and applied. Plato's most famous allegory is the allegory of the cave which he uses to clarify the implications of the metaphysical argument of the third section, and which contains the key to the plan and purpose of the *Republic*.

Before it can be appreciated properly the arguments leading up to it have to be understood. Socrates has been arguing that the true philosopher is not content to study a variety of beautiful objects but seeks to know what beauty is in itself, what is called the 'form' (*eidos*) or 'idea' (*idea*) of beauty (476). Plato's theory of forms or ideas has been the subject of much philosophical enquiry and discussion to which whole books have been devoted, but it need only be grasped in its essentials for the understanding of the argument of the *Republic*. There are forms of abstract things like beauty, goodness and justice, and of physical things like beds and tables. These forms transcend the phenomenal world of sense impression that is the world that we perceive through our senses of sight, hearing, touch, smell and taste. They exist apart and are eternal and unchanging. The phenomenal world in some way participates in this greater transcendent world of forms: a beautiful object is informed by beauty itself; a bed shares in the non-physical reality of the ideal bed. Only the forms are the objects of true knowledge. He who apprehends merely the particularities of the phenomenal world, apprehends mutable appearances, what seems to be true. He does not have knowledge but has opinion (*doxa*: the Greek word has the same root as the word *dokein*, to seem). The ultimate end of knowledge is the form of the good which gives meaning and value to everything in the universe. When asked to be more precise about this supreme reality Socrates confesses that he is unable to be so, and resorts to figurative language for further illustration, comparing the form of the good to the sun which gives visibility to the objects of the sensible world and the power of seeing to the eye. So the good makes the objects of thought (the forms) intelligible and gives the power of knowing to the mind (506d–509c). Plato then explores the distinction between the visible and intelligible worlds with the analogy of the divided line, through which he clarifies four sharply distinct mental states (the figure clarifies since in life they might not be so independent of one another). Opinion can be informed and true or illusory and false; knowledge may be of ultimate reality (the forms), or of a lesser reality which nevertheless transcends the world of sense (mathematical propositions). The four mental states are having illusions, having true beliefs and opinions, reasoning, and intelligence (509c–511e). These distinctions are clarified and further applied in the allegory of the cave which follows (514–17b).

All is clear from the outset. Socrates explains that the image is intended to picture the degrees to which we may be educated or ignorant.

The prisoners in the cave have been fettered since childhood in their underground cave and can only look in front of them. They have one fixed view from which they can see reflected on the wall opposite shadows of objects being carried through the cave by men walking on a road above them in front of which a wall has been built. Above and behind the road is a fire whose light casts the shadows of the objects which may be figures of men or animals in stone. An odd picture, remarks Glaucon, but Socrates replies that it is an image of our condition. For the prisoners, the shadows are the only realities. If one of them is let loose and compelled to turn his head and walk towards the fire, faced with the passing objects he will resist the new reality, taking refuge in the familiar. The light of the fire will hurt his eyes. If he is forced to make the ascent to the daylight, the process will be painful and he will at first not be able to see what is pointed out to him as real. Until his eyes grow accustomed to the light he will look at shadows and reflections, then at objects themselves, then at the heavens by night. The last thing he will be able to look at will be the sun itself. Then he will come to realise that the sun is the cause of all things. Reflecting upon his former life he will see that it was worthless. If he is made to come back to the cave, he will again be blinded and make a fool of himself in the eyes of his former fellows who will think the ascent has destroyed his eyesight and is not worth making. If anyone attempts to release them they will try to kill him.

Socrates then connects the image with what has gone before and proceeds to its interpretation likening the ascent into the upper world to the progress of the mind into the intelligible realm. At least this is his surmise but god alone knows whether it is true. The final thing to be perceived is the form of the good which is the cause of all things right and good (517bc).

Having delivered himself of his picture, Socrates then uses it to draw a number of conclusions. The philosopher with his eyes on the good will be reluctant to involve himself in human affairs, and may make a fool of himself if he is put on trial in the law courts where only the shadow of justice prevails. Education is not a question of giving sight to blind eyes but of turning round the mind itself so that it can look the right way. Procedures whereby this turning about can be achieved can be made into a professional skill. Some mental disciplines can be taught but the ability to think is innate, being useful or harmful depending on the direction in which it is exercised. Evil men may be intelligent but their intelligence serves evil ends and does not result in knowledge since they are slaves to appetites such as gluttony or sex. Society can never be properly governed by the uneducated, or by the purely intellectual. As law-givers we must ensure that philosophers go back down into the cave for the good of the whole. They must be as king-bees in the hive.

Once their sight is accustomed to the darkness they will see better than their fellows. Only those reluctant to govern who despise the shadow-boxing for the prizes of political power will govern well (517c–521b).

The allegory of the cave comes at the climax of a long investigation which has begun in Book Five (476e) into the character of the true philosopher and the nature of the knowledge that he seeks. Thereafter Plato considers the education necessary to equip the philosopher in his quest for knowledge of the good, for it is apparent that the educational programme prescribed earlier is merely preparatory; it is principally concerned with the development of moral character though by the end of it, it will be possible to decide who will have the capacity for further study. In the second phase of education Socrates first prescribes the study of the mathematical sciences to be followed finally by dialectic. To clarify the purpose of dialectic and mathematical study and to suggest the relation between them, Socrates makes further use of details from the allegory of the cave. In the visual realm (once out of the cave) the eye growing used to the light endeavours to look at living things themselves (as opposed to the images of them it had seen inside the cave), at the stars and finally at the sun itself. In the intellectual realm the mind through dialectic, the exercise of pure thought, seeks true knowledge of the eternal and immutable forms until finally it arrives at the summit of knowledge, the good itself (532). Socrates then illustrates the role of mathematical study in this intellectual endeavour. In the cave the released prisoners are turned round from shadows to the images that cast them and to the fire. Here they are still looking at man-made artefacts, the statues of men and images of animals that are carried along above the wall. Once out of the cave in the blinding light they are first able to see reflections in water of real things, whether animals or plants. Although only reflections, these have truer reality than the man-made objects seen in the cave. The reflections of real things represent the theorems and hypotheses of mathematics. Mathematical study leads to a knowledge of greater reality than anything in the world of sense since it deals with the reflections of reality, and is the best way of leading the mind upward to a vision of the highest order of reality, the forms that are known through dialectical reasoning (532cd).

The last reference to the cave comes when Socrates is giving a final review of the educational arrangements to be made for the philosopher rulers. After five years engaged in dialectic they will be compelled to go back into the cave for a further fifteen years (at the age of thirty-five) to hold military or other offices in order to have as much experience as those who have not passed beyond the cave. If they survive this experience of the cave intact they must then lift their gaze to that which illuminates all and use their knowledge of the good itself to direct and organise the state (540ab). With true knowledge of that which gives value and purpose to everything, the guardians will understand for themselves the philosophical principles upon which all legislation must be based. It is to be inferred that the guardians will instruct in true opinion those who are incapable of emerging from the cave by their own efforts, so that the lowest life of illusion may be avoided.

The allegory of the cave follows on naturally from the figures of the sun and the divided line and, like them, is used to clarify and illustrate metaphysical propositions that have been established in the reasoned argument of the dialogue. Unlike them, however, it serves to represent imaginatively not only Plato's whole view of life but also the powerful impulse that led him to write the *Republic*. Ordinary earthly life is lived in a benighted condition of ignorance from a fixed point of view in which the deluded soul is imprisoned without knowing it in a world of transient shadows. The impeding fetters are not simply intellectual, but are also moral. Nothing short of a radical turn-around of our mental and moral nature is needed. Enlightenment is a slow and painful process that is naturally and powerfully resisted by the ignorant and blind. Each stage of the upward journey into light is painful and difficult. But enlightenment *is* possible; eventually the released prisoner can behold the sun, although he is reluctant and has to be compelled at every stage. When in the beginning, after he has turned his head, he is told that all he has previously seen is illusory and he is cross-questioned about the objects passing before him, he is at a loss (in *aporia*), believing what he saw previously to be more real. The unmistakable allusion here to the Socratic method of refutation of conventional opinion (the *elenchus*) makes it clear that only the philosopher can effect the reformation necessary for enlightenment, though it is a dangerous proceeding, for the ignorant prisoners are liable to kill the man who attempts to lead them up the steep ascent.

The further allusion to Socrates and his death is a dramatic reminder of the power and brutality of ignorance (also embodied in the earlier illustrations of the sea captain and the great beast at 488, 493) from which Plato did not recoil in despair but which impelled him to write his Socratic dialogues in defence of all that Socrates had lived and died for. The writing of these dialogues for popular consumption itself exemplifies the moral duty that Plato lays upon the philosopher to descend again into the cave rather than to be content to cultivate his own garden without regard for the life of the community around him.

The allegory of the cave, therefore, is a figurative expression rich in meaning. It is a memorable image that gives concrete form to the difficult abstractions of the third section. Plato uses it both to clarify the significance of his preceding metaphysical argument and also to carry the argument forward as he applies the allegory and draws out its further significance. Later references to the cave in the third stage help to connect subsequent parts to the whole and thus both to clarify and to unify.

But the allegory of the cave is not only beautifully controlled to illustrate the argument of the third stage; it also comes at a climactic point in the overall plan of the *Republic* and illustrates the principle upon which the argument has been constructed. Plato began in the first stage with conventional views of justice from Polemarchus and Thrasymachus which were refuted by the Socratic *elenchus*. Socrates is here the man who is attempting to release the prisoner and effect his conversion. But Book One ends in a state of perplexity (*aporia*). The movement from illusion has not yet resulted in positive opinions about justice that are reflections of justice itself; in fact the illusory view of justice is put more forcefully by Glaucon and Adeimantus. The second stage culminates in the positive definition of justice given by Socrates at the end of Book Four and represents the upward movement from illusion to true opinion in which the released prisoner is turned towards the fire and contemplates the man-made artefacts that cast the shadows on the wall. But we are still in the cave, for we are dealing with civil institutions relating to education and the community of women and children, man-made constructions that correspond to the artefacts that cast shadows. The second stage shows the moral reformation necessary before there can be any general turn-about in the condition of the soul and shows how civil institutions must be made more conformable and conducive to the best in human nature. In the third stage, Socrates takes us out of the cave and into the light intimating just enough to open up new vistas to our unaccustomed sight. We first learn about the objects of true knowledge (the forms) and then about the means by which they can be known (dialectic by way of mathematical reasoning). The allegory of the cave therefore encapsulates all that has gone before. Its placing at the summit of the argument after Socrates has expatiated on the form of the good is a fine stroke of judgement on Plato's part. The form and the arrangement of the argument of the *Republic* are designed to ensure maximum ease of understanding. Under the comfortable illusion that we are eavesdropping on a spontaneous discussion the philosopher gradually reveals to us the way upward and ahead and guides us carefully through every stage. He does not take us to the summit, since the journey can only be made by the individual soul. But in figurative language he gives us a vision of what it might be (only god knows whether the figure is true, says Socrates at 517b) and shows us what practical measures must be taken if the vision is to be realised in experience.

But quite apart from all that has been said about its function in the third stage and in the argument of the *Republic* as a whole, the allegory of the cave is a masterly fictional invention that impresses itself deeply upon the mind independently of specific allegorical meaning attached to it and extracted from it by Plato. Long after the reader may have forgotten the precise argument or even the leading ideas of the *Republic*, the allegory of the cave is a memorable key to the whole tendency of Plato's thought and, in particular, to the sharp distinction he makes between the ideal and the phenomenal world. More than this, like the story of Adam and Eve in Genesis or the parables of Christ in the New Testament it has a general representative significance. It represents the tendency in Greek thought to find the source of human happiness and virtue in knowledge; it exalts the wise man as the enlightener and saviour of mankind and opens up the possibility of a steep and arduous upward road to truth through the application of human intelligence and the exercise of reason. This is the legacy of Greek humanism. We may contrast here the Judaeo-Christian tradition as represented by the two parts of the Bible. In Genesis the eating of the fruit of the tree of knowledge brings about the fall of man, the curse of consciousness and expulsion from Paradise. In the Old Testament righteousness depends not as in Plato upon the rule of human reason but upon faith in divine providence and obedience to the commandments of God revealed in the law of Moses and other prophets. It is the prophet, not the philosopher, who is exalted in Judaeism. In the new dispensation God intervenes in human history to redeem sinful man from the consequences of his fall by making the downward journey to earth and offering a way to salvation through faith in Christ. Faith, hope and love are the great Christian virtues exemplified in the life and together made possible by the death of Christ. In the life (and death) of Socrates (to which Plato's dialogues bear a relation similar to that between the Pauline epistles and the life and death of Christ) are exemplified the four cardinal virtues of the Greek world: wisdom, courage, temperance and justice. Both Christ and Socrates bear witness that natural unregenerate man needs to be turned away from the world and converted into new being. The old Adam is to be renewed by the saving power of the Christian Faith; the prisoners in the cave are to be educated by the virtue and energy of Greek Reason.

Part 4

Hints for study

THE GENERAL PHILOSOPHICAL BACKGROUND to Plato is briefly sketched in the Introduction. The summaries in Part 2 are designed to help the reader to follow the main lines of the argument. The commentary in Part 3 concentrates upon Plato's method in the *Republic*, on his organisation and illustration of the argument. The specimen essays that follow here further explore a characteristic of Plato's method, his use of myth. But if the student coming to Plato for the first time is really to grasp and to retain a grasp of Plato's argument, then an effort must be made to understand and to commit to memory certain key terms and basic ideas that together make up the essentials of Plato's thought as expressed in the *Republic* and other dialogues. What follows here is a brief recapitulation in concentrated form, for the sake of convenience with appropriate references to the text, of explanations that have already been given from time to time in the notes and commentary. Students are advised to make their own index by amplifying and extending what follows.

Some basic terms and elements in Plato's thought

Political terms

The title of the work in Greek is *Politeia* (whence polity in English), derived from *polis*, the city state (whence politics in English). The word basically means the system of government or the constitution of the state, and can be used to mean a well-ordered commonwealth. It is translated into Latin by the word *Respublica* from which comes the English title *Republic*. Plato calls his ideal state a *paradeigma* (592b), a pattern, model, example or paradigm. He also calls it *Kallipolis* (527c), 'Fair city' from *Kallos*, beauty. Various states are described in the *Republic*. The most primitive is the necessary state (369–72) which Glaucon calls the city of pigs (372d). Then comes the civilised or luxurious state (372d) which is similar to the unreformed Athenian society of Plato's day. Later in the book Plato envisages a possible decline from the ideal state first to timocracy derived from *kratos*, power, and *time*, honour (545c). After timocracy comes oligarchy from *arche*, rule, and *oligoi*, the few (551c). The opposite of the few is the many, *hoi polloi*, a phrase that has entered general consciousness. Oligarchy yields to democracy in which power lies with the *demos*, the people (555b). Finally comes tyranny from the Greek word for a single ruler, *tyrannos* (562).

Justice and the four virtues

The alternative title of the *Republic* in antiquity is 'Concerning *dikaiosyne*'. The word is usually translated into English as justice, which suggests the legal associations of the word but does not fully convey its moral significance. It concerns the individual's conduct as it affects others; all that others have a right to expect of the individual and what the individual has a right to expect from them. It can be translated by the old-fashioned English word righteousness, embracing right conduct and the moral life. It can be characteristic of the individual or the community. Preliminary definitions are given at 331cde. Thrasymachus starts to give his point of view at 338c. Glaucon restates Thrasymachus's view at 358e. Socrates defines justice in the state at 427d and 433, and justice in the individual at 443e. Justice is one of the four cardinal virtues of the ancient world (427e). The other three are wisdom, courage and temperance (429). *Sophia*, wisdom, is also the word for intelligence and skill. The wisdom of the city resides in the knowledge of the guardians (429). Wisdom in the individual is the rule of reason (442c); *philosophia* is the love of wisdom. The guardians are to be philosophers. What constitutes the true philosopher is a major part of the dialogue from 474 to 521. Courage, *andreia*, is a development from manliness, derived from *aner-andros*, a man. Courage in the state is located in that part which defends it and is also the defence and safe-keeping of established values (429). In the individual it is defined as holding fast to a rational idea of what is to be feared, irrespective of emotional considerations (442b). The Greek word *sophrosyne* (402c) is sometimes translated as soundness of mind, sobriety or good sense. It is defined as control of desires at 430e whence it is usually taken to mean self-discipline or temperance. It is present in the state when the desires of the majority are controlled by the wisdom of the ruling minority (431cd). It is represented by the harmony that exists between the various parts of the state when they are in proper relation (432). In the individual it is a comparable harmony between the various parts of the soul under the rule of reason (442cd). Justice in the state (427d) and in the individual (443e) is the principle which makes this temperance possible; it is an extension of the principle of the division of labour upon which society is based in the first place (369–70), the principle whereby each class in the state or each part of the soul fulfils its own function without trespassing upon the functions of the other two.

Education

The Greek word for the upbringing and training of children is *paideia*, derived from *paides*, children. It is used to mean enlightenment at the opening of the allegory of the cave (514). Hellenic education had two parts which were designed to complement one another to produce the all-round man. The first, *mousike paideia* (376e), relates not only to music but to all the arts over which the nine Muses presided. It includes literature and history and all the liberal arts, and educated the spiritual and mental faculties. The second, *gymnastike paideia* (376e), is physical education. The word *gymnos* means naked. The Greeks exercised naked in their gymnasia. In the ideal state Plato regards all that precedes dialectic as *propaedia* (536d), preliminary education (the prefix *pro* means before).

The three classes in the state and the three parts of the soul

The need for a guardian class to defend the state is established at 374–6. Plato's word for guardian is *phylax* (from which the English word prophylactic is derived). The guardians are fully defined at 414b where they are distinguished from the second class of *epikouroi* which literally means helpers and is generally translated as auxiliaries. Plato divides the state into three classes (434c) but does not use one word to cover his third class. In the myth of metals they are workers and farmers (415). Later they are workers and businessmen (434c). Arguing from the state to the individual, Plato finds three corresponding elements in the individual soul (435b). The word *psyche* is used by Plato for both mind and soul. It is essentially non-physical and survives the death of the body (*soma*). The adjective psychosomatic is made up of these two Greek words. The meaning of psyche in the words psychoanalysis and psychical conveys in part what is referred to in the Greek. The three parts of the soul are the rational part, *to logistikon*, from *logos* meaning word discourse or reason (439d), *to thumoeides*, the spirited or assertive element, from *thumos*, the spirit (439e), and the appetitive element, *to epithumetikon*, from *epithumia*, appetite or desire (439d). The relation between them is discussed at 434–40. There is a correspondence between the three classes of the state and the three parts of the soul. In the ideal state, the guardians rule; in the harmonious soul reason rules spirit and appetite. Each part of the soul has its own pleasure, *hedone* (580, whence hedonism). The fate of the soul is the subject of the myth of Er (614b).

The forms, knowledge and opinion, poetry

The theory of forms and ideas is nowhere set out systematically either in the *Republic* or elsewhere in Plato. It is explained according to the needs of the argument at the time (see especially passages beginning at 476 and 596). The expressions Platonic form and Platonic idea (sometimes Platonic ideal) meaning the pure abstract essence of something have entered general consciousness. Plato uses the words *eidos* (form) and *idea* (idea) interchangeably and no clear philosophical distinction can be drawn between the words which are rendered as form or idea according to the preference of the translator. Though the word form may have concrete associations, Plato clearly has in mind an abstract entity that exists independently of the material world. The forms are metaphysical (derived from *meta*, after, and *physis*, nature). The word idea on the other hand may suggest inappropriate subjectivity. His abstractions are unchanging and eternal having a transcendent existence independent of the mind that comes to know them. A form is pure, excluding its opposite; beauty and ugliness are two (475e). There may be forms or ideas of both concrete things such as beds and tables (596b), and of abstractions like beauty in itself or justice in itself (476). Only these forms are the objects of true knowledge (*gnosis* or *episteme* from which epistemology, the science of knowledge). Particular examples of beautiful things or the material objects that we perceive with our senses in the phenomenal world (from *phainomena*, things that seem to be) share in the transcendent form (476d) but are not themselves the objects of true knowledge. Our apprehension of the shifting phenomenal world of appearances is called *doxa* (476−80) which is translated usually as opinion and sometimes as belief. The word is derived from the verb *dokein*, to seem. Opinion lies between knowledge and ignorance (*agnoia* (477b), whence agnostic). Knowledge is related to what is, to being. From *onta*, meaning things that are (the neuter plural of the present participle of the verb *einai* to be) is derived ontology, the science of being. Being or reality for Plato subsists in the forms and ultimate reality, the ground of all being, is the form of the good. This is not precisely defined, but the comparison of the form of the good to the sun (507−9) clarifies the meaning of Plato's conception.

The figure of the divided line (509e−511) further extends the distinction between knowledge and opinion to distinguish four mental states, each with its corresponding apprehension of reality. Knowledge is subdivided into *noesis*, intelligence, and *dianoia*, variously translated as thought, mathematical intelligence and reason which operates upon the assumptions (Plato's word is *hypotheses*, 510b) of mathematics. The first stage of the advanced education of the guardian rulers is concerned with mathematical study (524−31c). From mathematical study, the guardians move to dialectic (511c, 531d – 534e). Through dialectic the mind moves from assumptions, not simply to conclusions as in mathematics, but to a first principle (*anupothetos arche*, 510b and 511b) and to knowledge of the forms themselves (511b). The ultimate object of knowledge is the form of the good.

In the inferior realm *doxa* is similarly divided into two states, the lowest of which is *eikasia* (511d) usually translated as illusion, in which shadows and reflections are taken to be real. This is the condition of an undiscriminating acceptance of commonplace opinion and conventional belief, the state of the ignorant majority. A higher state than this which is more reliable and informed but which is nevertheless based as far as the believer is concerned upon opinion rather than knowledge is called *pistis* (511e), belief. The first stage of the education of the guardians in which the existing Hellenic education is reformed to bring it into line with the philosophical principles upon which the ideal state is to be founded represents the movement in the *Republic* from illusion to true opinion. In the ideal state itself the philosopher rulers who have true knowledge will educate the young and those incapable of reaching true knowledge for themselves in true opinion that conforms to knowledge (590d). The relation between these various states of mind, the nature of its upward journey from one state to another and the role of the philosopher in this process are further clarified in the allegory of the cave (514–18).

Poetry (*poiesis*) belongs to the lower realm (Plato's word for image is *eikon* (487e, 515) which is related to *eikasia*) and must be made to conform to higher reality. Plato has one word for both fiction and falsehood, *pseudos* (414b). He objects to poetry as a mode of truth because it is a representation (his word is *mimesis* which is sometimes translated imitation, 595c) of the world of appearances which is itself a distorted reflection of the transcendent world of unchanging and eternal forms. Its images are therefore at two removes from reality. This objection is called the epistemological objection. Plato similarly objects to the education provided by the sophists (the root meaning of *sophistes* is an adept and expert, a man of skill) who simply make a science of common opinion (492).

Related works of Plato and others

The *Apology* is particularly to be recommended for its portrait of Socrates and the defence he gave of his life at his trial. In *The Last Days of Socrates*, published by Penguin Books, it is conveniently included alongside the *Crito* and the *Phaedo*, two other early dialogues that purport to represent conversations between Socrates and his friends just before his death. The *Timaeus* begins as a continuation of the *Republic* and includes Plato's account of creation. The political thought of the *Republic* is considerably modified in the *Laws* written by Plato later in life. After the *Republic*, the most famous of Plato's dialogues is probably the *Symposium*, on the nature of love. *The Collected Dialogues of Plato including the Letters* translated into English by various hands is conveniently available in one volume with introduction and prefatory notes, edited by Edith Hamilton and Huntingdon Cairns and published by Princeton University Press. The volume has an excellent general index of more than one hundred pages covering the whole of Plato's work.

In the literature of antiquity Plato's *Republic* may be put alongside the political thought of his pupil Aristotle in his *Politics* and the Roman Cicero in his *De Republica*. A Christian comparison can be made with the *De Civitate Dei* (the City of God, like Kallipolis, is a pattern laid up in heaven) by Augustine of Hippo (AD345–430). In the Renaissance, *Utopia* (1516), by the humanist Thomas More (1478–1535), challenges comparison with the *Republic*. *New Atlantis* (1626), by the philosopher Francis Bacon (1561–1626), carries on the tradition. Plato had made use of the Atlantis myth in the *Timaeus* and the *Critias*.

Translations and commentaries

Most of the editions of the *Republic* likely to be used by modern students contain introductory material and notes that are useful for the general reader and which have necessarily been reduplicated to some extent in this volume. The most literal version is that of Shorey in the bilingual Loeb edition which has the Greek text with a translation on the facing page. This edition has a useful index as well as an introduction and notes. The Everyman version by Lindsay also follows the Greek closely but is more idiomatic than Shorey. At the beginning it contains a useful analysis of the argument made by the translator. The introduction and notes written by a subsequent editor are designed for the general student of philosophy. Finding fault with versions written in unidiomatic English that follow the Greek with laborious faithfulness to the letter of Plato's meaning at the expense of its sense and spirit, Cornford in his translation published by Oxford University Press writes paraphrastically and omits some of the more perfunctory conversational interjections of Socrates's respondents. Many of Plato's quotations from the poets are omitted. In other respects this translation simplifies the text from time to time, but Cornford is careful to alert his readers to such changes and omissions. He abandons the ten-book division and follows the more obvious division of the argument referred to in the present commentary (page 51), with subdivisions of his own. In addition to the footnotes, each section is prefaced by an admirably clear introduction, and there is a useful index. The Penguin translation by Lee is written in modern colloquial English. The translator has divided the argument into eleven parts with subdivisions. Each part is introduced with a summary and discussion. There is a long introduction and footnotes, appendices and a more extensive bibliography than in other editions referred to here.

For those who understand Greek the celebrated edition (published in 1902) by the Cambridge classical scholar James Adam (1860–1907) contains a full commentary and full indices to both text and commentary. The Oxford classical scholar R.L. Nettleship (1848–92) so arranged his *Lectures on Plato's Republic* (published posthumously in 1897) as to give a continuous running commentary. His pupil and subsequent student of philosophy Bernard Bosanquet (1848–1923) produced a detailed point-by-point commentary for English readers in *A Companion to Plato's Republic* (1895). All these old commentaries of which full details are given in Part 5 contain material that is useful for the modern student. The extent to which they are influenced by current philosophic preoccupations and an idealising attitude to Plato is discussed by F.M. Turner, in 'The Victorian Platonic Revival' in *The Greek Heritage in Victorian Britain* (1981). Included in the volume is comment upon the famous Victorian translator of Plato, Benjamin Jowett (1817–93), Master of Balliol College, Oxford.

Criticism of Plato

The *Republic* has always been a controversial document. The wisdom of Plato's prescriptions for the ideal state was immediately questioned, principally upon grounds of practicability, by Plato's pupil Aristotle in his *Politics* (1260–4). He finds fault with Plato's proposals to abolish the family and ownership of private property among the ruling guardians, which he believes to be neither practicable nor desirable. He attacks the basic premise from which Plato argues that the highest unity of a state is its highest good, insisting that plurality is the nature of a state. He argues that Plato does not take account of the facts of human nature; present evils and abuses in society spring not from private ownership and the family but from basic human wickedness. He also finds gaps in Plato's provisions, noting that there are no arrangements for the majority, the third class of artisans and farmers. Contemplating the class structure of Plato's city, Aristotle sees two states in one, a recipe for strife. Arguing that the whole cannot be happy unless all or at least some of its parts are happy, he finds fault with Plato's argument that the happiness of the guardians is to be sacrificed to the happiness of the whole, clearly believing along with Glaucon (419) that

Plato's ideal city will be a dismal place in which to live. It has long been argued that Aristotle's whole philosophical outlook developed in reaction to Plato, and in the *Poetics* Aristotle puts forward a theory of poetry which indirectly counters Plato's objections.

For the German philosopher G.W.F. Hegel (1770–1831) Plato is not ideal enough. Though he founds his state upon reason, he does not allow for reason as manifested in individual conscience, in subjective freedom. The attack on Plato has been most strenuous in the twentieth century. In *The Open Society and its Enemies* (1945), Karl Popper (*b*.1902) sees Plato as the enemy of liberal and humanitarian ideals and as the prophet of totalitarianism.

But it is not only Plato's thought that has been criticised; his method has also been called into question. Hegel found the mixture of poetry and philosophy disconcerting. Plato's method of conducting his argument, in particular his use of analogy, has also been criticised (by Aristotle in *Politics*, 1264b). Plato makes frequent use of analogies drawn from the animal world, comparing the guardians to watchdogs (375), for example, or basing his argument for relations between the sexes on analogies with the breeding of animals (457–61). He also makes frequent use of analogies drawn from the practical arts (called in Greek *technai*; see, for example, 332–6) on the basis that politics and education are themselves teachable skills like medicine or seamanship, subject to discernible rules. The validity of both kinds of analogy is often questionable.

Some questions and answers

(1) What are the advantages and disadvantages of the dialogue form in the *Republic*?

(2) How does Plato characterise Socrates in the *Republic*?

(3) 'Nowhere in Plato is there deeper irony or greater wealth of humour or imagery or more dramatic power' (Benjamin Jowett). Identify these characteristics and assess their contribution to Plato's *Republic*.

(4) 'Thrasymachus is refuted only because Plato unfairly attributes to him admissions he need never have made.' Is this fair criticism?

(5) 'Having set out to discuss the just man and justice, he adduced a city by way of illustration and then expatiated at much greater length on the constitution of the state. . . . He is criticised, not altogether unfairly, on the ground that this matter has nothing to do with the subject under discussion and throws not a glimmer of light upon it' (the verdict of the Greek orator and popular philosopher Dion Chrysostom (*c*.AD40–112), VII, 130).

(6) 'The only problem about the sun, the line and the cave is to explain

why Plato thought it necessary to say the same thing in three different ways.'

(7) Account for Plato's hostility to (a) democracy, (b) poetry.

(8) 'The *Republic* is not a treatise on politics but the finest treatise on education ever written' (the judgement of the French philosopher Jean Jacques Rousseau (1712−78)). Is it possible to make this distinction and if so, is Plato's educational thinking of more interest and value than his political thinking?

(9) How might Plato have responded to the criticism of his political thought made by Aristotle in his *Politics* (1200−64)?

(10) 'Our modern objection to Plato is that he is much too realistic in his analysis of human nature' (R.H.S. Crossman (1907−74), *Plato Today*).

Specimen essay

What is the function of myth in Plato's *Republic*?

The myth of metals (414b−415d)

Much of Plato's discussion of the early education of the guardians is concerned to modify the existing Hellenic education in which poetry and mythology played a major part. His treatment of poetry and that of mythology go hand in hand since Plato believed that traditional mythology was largely the invention of the poets (377d). He does not banish poetry and the stories that poets tell altogether (the Greek word for story is *mythos*). Only what is theologically and morally unsound is to be banished. Poems on suitable subjects and myths that are morally edifying continue to play a leading role in the education of the young (376e, 392b). Plato is not, therefore, opposed to fiction as such, and apart from its role in the education of the children, he assigns to it a useful function in the consciousness of the state at large.

Remarking that it is difficult to know the truth about the distant past, Socrates acknowledges that fictions can be invented which represent the nearest approximation to that truth (382cd). Such a fiction Socrates himself invents when he provides a foundation myth for his ideal state (414b−415d).

The myth is introduced after Socrates has completed his account of the cultural and physical education of the guardians and has drawn for the first time the distinction between the guardians and the auxiliaries. Socrates is somewhat shamefaced about introducing what he calls his 'noble fiction'; it is the sort of story that poets have persuaded people happened once upon a time, but which has not happened recently and which is not likely to happen again (414c).

Everybody is to be persuaded that the education just described happened only in a dream; in reality all were moulded and fashioned along with their equipment and arms in the womb of the earth who brought them forth complete. The citizens are therefore all brothers born of one mother whom they are bound to protect. The Athenians, like the citizens of many other Greek states, popularly believed themselves to be the indigenous inhabitants of Athens descended from earth-born 'autochthonous' parents (from *auto* itself and *chthon* earth), so that Plato is adapting traditional belief. Although they are brothers in the ideal state, god in fashioning the citizens has added gold to the making of those destined to be rulers, silver to the auxiliaries and iron and bronze to the lower orders of society. The citizens will generally produce children of the same metal as their parents, but occasionally silver children may be born to gold parents and vice versa; similarly bronze parents may produce a more precious child. In these cases it is imperative that such children be promoted or degraded into their appropriate class, as there is a prophecy to the effect that the state will perish when silver and bronze become its guardians. It will be difficult to convince the first generation of citizens but subsequent generations may come to believe it.

The magnificent myth is, therefore, for the whole community, including the guardians and auxiliaries, so that it is not to be interpreted simply as a device of propaganda whereby power is to be maintained in the hands of the ruling class. The political purpose of the myth in the ideal state is to ensure social cohesion by fostering a sense of common origin, identity, and interest in all its citizens and at the same to ensure that the principle of division between the classes is strictly maintained by the flexible movement upwards and downwards between classes according to natural endowment. In the argument of the *Republic* the myth makes it graphically clear that Plato's ideal state is an aristocracy based not upon birth and inherited position but upon intrinsic merit. The myth therefore has a twofold didactic function, the first political in the ideal state and the second artistic in the development of the argument. In both respects Plato realistically acknowledges the power and appeal of myth over the minds, hearts, and imaginations of men.

As a political device the foundation myth is rather awkwardly introduced because apart from the question of its credibility such a myth does not of course come into existence instantly any more than the ideal state is born in an instant of time in fully developed form. Just as the decline of the state in Book Eight is not meant to reflect a historical reality but is to illustrate a logical (and psychological) degeneration, so here the way in which the foundation myth is introduced into the ideal state is not meant to illustrate a historical actuality or even possibility but serves a logical purpose in the development of the argument.

As an artistic device serving the argument, the myth is both cunningly wrought and cunningly placed. It comes at the precise moment when Socrates founds his state and, rather than merely clarifying what has gone before, the myth actually establishes and extends our conception of the principles upon which the newly formed state is being founded and must be maintained. With the fiction of the earth-born citizens, Plato, by a sleight of hand, is able to introduce his ideal state in an instant without having to say in practice how it is possible to go from present reality to the ideal. In an elegant transition, after he has finished with the foundation myth, Socrates leads his earth-born citizens into their new city under the leadership of their rulers (415e). Now that it has served its purpose, there is no further reference to it. When Plato later comes to develop fully the philosophic principles upon which the ideal state is founded, we have moved from myth to reason and dialectic.

The myth of Er (614–21)

Plato also uses myth to push philosophical enquiry beyond the point at which certain knowledge is possible. The myth of Er at the close of the *Republic* is an imaginative vision of the life and destiny of the soul. Plato introduces this grand vision at the conclusion of his work to set his philosophy in the widest possible perspective. In offering rewards for the just after death (as well as punishments for the unjust) the myth with its eschatological dimension (from the Greek *eschata*, last things) is intended to offer an inducement to the good life which Plato has been urging from the beginning.

The myth comes after Socrates has offered demonstrative proof in argument for the immortality of the soul. He has argued that the number of souls in the universe is always constant and that the soul can only be seen for what it is if it is viewed apart from the body and from those factors in human life which oppress it and weigh it down. Although he has shown that justice is its own reward, Socrates nevertheless wishes to demonstrate that virtue is rewarded by the gods not only in this life but in the life to come. Socrates tells the tale of Er, a soldier killed in battle who is allowed to come alive again after he has seen what happens to the soul after death. Er first travels to a meadow where he hears the experiences of other souls who have completed the thousand-year period of reward or punishment. Every wrong on earth is punished tenfold while the good are similarly rewarded. Souls beyond redemption like the tyrant (whom Thrasymachus had pronounced the most fortunate of men) are flung into Tartarus, a place of eternal punishment. After spending seven days in the meadow Er rises up with the souls that had returned from the thousand-year journey to a place from which the whole structue of the universe can be seen. Here he describes the spindle of Necessity from which all the orbits of the planets and the fixed stars revolve. He describes the music of the spheres and the three Fates who sing of things past, things present and things to come. Here the souls are required to choose new lives. The order of choosing is determined by lot, but there are more lives than souls so that even he who draws the last lot has a measure of choice. Er witnesses the souls making their fateful choices. Most souls choose a life comparable to their previous experience. There is interchange between the human and animal world. After the choice, the Fates give each soul its accompanying genius. The choice is finally ratified by Necessity. Thereafter the souls drink the waters of Lethe and so forget their knowledge of what awaits them when they are immediately carried upwards to be born.

Most of the ideas in the myth of Er, such as the doctrine of judgement after death, have a long history in Greek religious thought and belief. The doctrines of reincarnation and purification in a cycle of lives are particularly associated with the Pythagoreans. Most of the topographical details of the myth are probably inherited too. They are deliberately vague, since Plato needs only enough concrete detail to provide a framework for certain leading ideas. Striking is the emphasis upon necessity; the spindle of Necessity determines the structure of the universe and ratifies the choice of life made by the soul. But equally striking (and this is Plato's emphasis and not a feature of his sources) is the freedom of choice allowed to the individual soul in choosing the form of its earthly life. This freedom is not absolute since the order of choice is determined by lot. But even those unlucky in the lottery may nevertheless choose well (619e). This mixture expresses a reality in which each person's life is partly determined by factors beyond his or her control and partly determined by moral choice, and takes account of the role of chance (or fate) and free will in determining the character and quality of the individual's life. When it comes to making the choice of life, the individual is free to choose from the patterns available, and is therefore responsible for the fatal decision. Hence the necessity, urges Socrates, of knowing the correct basis upon which a good life is to be distinguished from a bad one and of seeking out the guidance of the philosopher (618c). In practice Er observes that many choose on the basis of inadequate knowledge. Even those who·had previously led good lives make bad choices because their previous goodness has been an expression of habit or convention rather than the conscious moral choice arrived at through philosophic self-examination. Those who have suffered in earthly life are more likely to choose wisely as a result of their previous bad experiences.

The myth is a graphic representation of Plato's belief in a universe governed by unalterable law in which there is nevertheless individual freedom of moral choice. The myth dramatises the fateful character of

moral choice in which the destiny of the soul is at stake, but it nevertheless is not without hope for human kind: 'Even for the last comer, if he
chooses wisely and lives strenuously, there remains a life that is accept-
able and no bad choice. Let him who chooses first take heed, and him
who chooses last not be discouraged' (619b). Such are the character
and legacy of Greek humanism.

Part 5

Suggestions for further reading

The text, translations and commentaries

Plato, Vol. IV, edited by J. Burnet, Oxford Classical Texts, Clarendon Press, Oxford, 1962.

The Republic of Plato, edited with critical notes, commentary and appendices by James Adam, 2 vols, Cambridge University Press, Cambridge, 1902; second edn, 1965.

Plato V: The Republic, with an English translation by Paul Shorey, Loeb Classical Library, 2 vols, Harvard University Press, Cambridge, Mass.; Heinemann, London, 1930–5.

Plato: The Republic, translated by A.D. Lindsay, with introduction and notes by Renford Bamborough, Everyman's Library, J.M. Dent & Sons, London, 1976.

The Republic of Plato, translated with introduction and notes by F.M. Cornford, Clarendon Press, Oxford, 1941 (paperback 1945).

Plato: The Republic, translated with an introduction by Desmond Lee, Penguin Books, Harmondsworth, 1955; second edn (revised), 1974.

The Collected Dialogues of Plato including the Letters, edited with introduction and prefatory notes by Edith Hamilton and Huntingdon Cairns, Princeton University Press, Princeton, N.J., 1961.

BOSANQUET, BERNARD: *A Companion to Plato's Republic for English Readers*, second edn, Rivington Percival, London, 1895.

NETTLESHIP, R.L.: Lectures on the Republic of Plato, Macmillan paperback, London, 1963 (first published in 1897).

General works

COPLESTON, F.: History of Philosophy, Vol. I, *Greece and Rome*, Burns and Oates Ltd., London, 1946.

CORNFORD, F.M.: Before and After Socrates, Cambridge University Press, Cambridge, 1932.

CROSSMAN, R.H.S.: *Plato Today*, George Allen & Unwin, revised second edn, London 1959.

FIELD, G.C.: *Plato and his Contemporaries*, Methuen, London 1948.

FINLEY, M.I.: *The Ancient Greeks*, Penguin Books, Harmondsworth, 1966.

The Oxford Classical Dictionary, edited by N.G.L. Hammond and H.H. Scullard, Clarendon Press, Oxford, second edn, 1970.

POPPER, K.R.: *The Open Society and its Enemies*, Vol. 1: *The Spell of Plato*, Routledge & Kegan Paul, London, 1946.

TURNER, F.M.: *The Greek Heritage in Victorian Britain*, Yale University Press, New Haven and London, 1981 (chapters on Socrates and Plato).

The author of these notes

ROBIN SOWERBY was educated at St Catharine's College, Cambridge, where he read Classics and English. Since 1972 he has been a lecturer in the Department of English Studies at Stirling University, from which he spent a year (1984–5) on secondment to the National University of Singapore. He is also the author of York Notes on *The Aeneid* and *The Iliad*.

YORK NOTES

The first 200 titles

	Series number
CHINUA ACHEBE	
A Man of the People	(116)
Arrow of God	(92)
Things Fall Apart	(96)
ELECHI AMADI	
The Concubine	(139)
JOHN ARDEN	
Serjeant Musgrave's Dance	(159)
AYI KWEI ARMAH	
The Beautyful Ones Are Not Yet Born	(154)
JANE AUSTEN	
Emma	(142)
Northanger Abbey	(1)
Persuasion	(69)
Pride and Prejudice	(62)
Sense and Sensibility	(91)
SAMUEL BECKETT	
Waiting for Godot	(115)
SAUL BELLOW	
Henderson, The Rain King	(146)
ARNOLD BENNETT	
Anna of the Five Towns	(144)
WILLIAM BLAKE	
Songs of Innocence, Songs of Experience	(173)
ROBERT BOLT	
A Man For All Seasons	(51)
CHARLOTTE BRONTË	
Jane Eyre	(21)
EMILY BRONTË	
Wuthering Heights	(43)
JOHN BUCHAN	
The Thirty-Nine Steps	(89)
ALBERT CAMUS	
L'Etranger (The Outsider)	(46)
GEOFFREY CHAUCER	
Prologue to the Canterbury Tales	(30)
The Franklin's Tale	(78)
The Knight's Tale	(97)
The Merchant's Tale	(193)
The Miller's Tale	(192)
The Nun's Priest's Tale	(16)
The Pardoner's Tale	(50)
The Wife of Bath's Tale	(109)
Troilus and Criseyde	(198)
SAMUEL TAYLOR COLERIDGE	
Selected Poems	(165)
WILKIE COLLINS	
The Woman in White	(182)
SIR ARTHUR CONAN DOYLE	
The Hound of the Baskervilles	(53)
JOSEPH CONRAD	
Heart of Darkness	(152)
Lord Jim	(150)
Nostromo	(68)
The Secret Agent	(138)
Youth and *Typhoon*	(100)
DANIEL DEFOE	
Moll Flanders	(153)
Robinson Crusoe	(28)
CHARLES DICKENS	
A Tale of Two Cities	(70)
Bleak House	(183)
David Copperfield	(9)
Great Expectations	(66)
Nicholas Nickleby	(161)
Oliver Twist	(101)
The Pickwick Papers	(110)

	Series number
JOHN DONNE	
Selected Poems	(199)
THEODORE DREISER	
Sister Carrie	(179)
GEORGE ELIOT	
Adam Bede	(14)
Silas Marner	(98)
The Mill on the Floss	(29)
T. S. ELIOT	
Four Quartets	(167)
Murder in the Cathedral	(149)
Selected Poems	(155)
The Waste Land	(45)
WILLIAM FAULKNER	
Absalom, Absalom!	(124)
As I Lay Dying	(44)
Go Down, Moses	(163)
The Sound and the Fury	(136)
HENRY FIELDING	
Joseph Andrews	(105)
Tom Jones	(113)
F. SCOTT FITZGERALD	
The Great Gatsby	(8)
E. M. FORSTER	
A Passage to India	(151)
ATHOL FUGARD	
Selected Plays	(63)
MRS GASKELL	
North and South	(60)
WILLIAM GOLDING	
Lord of the Flies	(77)
OLIVER GOLDSMITH	
She Stoops to Conquer	(71)
The Vicar of Wakefield	(79)
GRAHAM GREENE	
The Power and the Glory	(188)
THOMAS HARDY	
Far From the Madding Crowd	(174)
Jude the Obscure	(6)
Selected Poems	(169)
Tess of the D'Urbervilles	(80)
The Mayor of Casterbridge	(39)
The Return of the Native	(20)
The Trumpet Major	(74)
The Woodlanders	(160)
Under the Greenwood Tree	(129)
L. P. HARTLEY	
The Go-Between	(36)
The Shrimp and the Anemone	(123)
NATHANIEL HAWTHORNE	
The Scarlet Letter	(134)
ERNEST HEMINGWAY	
A Farewell to Arms	(145)
For Whom the Bell Tolls	(95)
The Old Man and the Sea	(11)
HERMANN HESSE	
Steppenwolf	(135)
BARRY HINES	
Kes	(189)
ANTHONY HOPE	
The Prisoner of Zenda	(88)
WILLIAM DEAN HOWELLS	
The Rise of Silas Lapham	(175)
RICHARD HUGHES	
A High Wind in Jamaica	(17)
THOMAS HUGHES	
Tom Brown's Schooldays	(2)